(Nearly) Total Recall

A Guide to a Better Memory at Any Age

DANIELLE C. LAPP

THE PORTABLE STANFORD is a book series
sponsored by the Stanford Alumni Association.
The series is designed to bring the widest possible
sampling of Stanford's intellectual resources into the
homes of alumni. It includes books based on current
research as well as books that deal with philosophical
issues, which by their nature reflect to a greater degree
the personal views of their authors.

THE PORTABLE STANFORD BOOK SERIES
Stanford Alumni Association
Bowman Alumni House
Stanford, California 94305-4005

Library of Congress Catalog Card
Number: 92-061793
ISBN: 0-916318-51-6

10 9 8 7 6 5 4 3 2 1

The
Portable Stanford
Book Series

Published by the
Stanford Alumni Association

Editor-in-chief: Della van Heyst
Series Editor and Manager: Bruce Goldman
Book Design/Production Manager: Amy Pilkington
Cover Design: Elaine Kwong
Cover Art: Salvador Dali

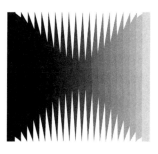

To Jerry, who always makes it happen.

ACKNOWLEDGMENTS

"Gratitude is the heart's memory."

Many thanks to all those who have helped bring this project to completion. In particular, I am grateful to Dr. Jerome Yesavage for his support and input in the Medical Issues section. My editor, Bruce Goldman, proved to be a treasure of precision and thoroughness, improving my text with open mind and clarity of purpose. Production manager Amy Pilkington also deserves praise for her kindness and efficacy, which made our work a breeze.

TABLE OF CONTENTS

Mini-Glossary

While most of the boldfaced terms you will encounter in this book are self-explanatory, a few are listed here for easy reference:

- **automatic gestures** = habitual routines (like locking a car door) that, because they are performed without awareness or conscious thinking, may not be recorded into memory and may therefore not be recalled later on.

- **depth of processing** = the mental strategies and processes—such as visualization, image-association, verbal elaboration, summarization, and review—that are indispensable to the recording of a good memory trace.

- **image-association** = the conscious pairing of two mental images, so that the sight or recall of one will trigger recall of the other.

- **mnemonics, mnemonic systems** = cues to trigger recall of information.

- **selective attention** = defining what you want to remember, why, and for how long.

- **verbal elaboration** = comments, analysis, judgments, etc., that act to enhance the recording of a memory trace.

FOREWORD

In this book I propose to answer as many questions as the curious reader might raise about memory. I have selected those questions I consider essential, and tried to anticipate others. Since you will no doubt choose to read first the ones that interest you, I have attempted to make each answer self-contained, so that you can look at the table of contents and go right to the question on your mind.

The answers to these questions are not absolute: They reflect the present knowledge on the subject, and an empirical approach based on the results obtained in the context of research on memory training. In my first book, *Don't Forget! Easy Exercises for a*

Better Memory at Any Age, I outlined a method proven to be effective in our research studies on memory and aging, with an emphasis on exercises. But busy people often have no inclination to do exercises, and want specific answers to specific questions. Moreover, research shows that improvement in memory-related performance is maximized when individuals get actively involved and devise their own adaptations and strategies.

The question-and-answer format has its limitations. Attempts to give succinct answers often result in apparent simplification. However, it would be advisable not to dismiss *a priori* simple solutions: Many prove efficient in spite of their banal evidence. Some people refuse help when they judge the suggestion too simplistic. As the philosopher Wittgenstein used to say: "It is always difficult to accept simple solutions to complex problems." Interestingly, I have found the greatest resistance to mnemonic techniques among intellectuals. This may be partly due to the fact that many of these techniques shun abstraction and rely on imagery, imagination, and emotional involvement.

In this book, I often give personal examples such as remembering recipes or other procedures by acquiring principles that are constantly rehearsed, as is the case in cooking, gardening, teaching, or writing. All the principles of good retention are thus integrated in an effortless manner, because they are reviewed in numerous different contexts. This approach mimics empirical learning in everyday life: Did you know that one needs to encounter a new word six different times in context to fully integrate it into vocabulary? Only then is it assimilated.

The state of research on memory does not always provide answers to the questions "why?", but memory processes have been studied enough to give satisfactory answers to the questions "how?". This practical guide focuses on the "hows": How does it work? How can we facilitate recall? I have made every effort to keep it free of scientific jargon. When they must be invoked, key concepts such as "mental imagery" or "depth of processing" are explained and illustrated. Several strategies are offered for the reader to choose from. The method we shall use has been proving its worth for more than thirteen years in double-blind, controlled studies led by Dr. Jerome Yesavage of Stanford University School of Medicine's Department of Psychiatry. In 1978 I started working with him on pilot studies in which we trained normal healthy people over 55 years of age with the standard mnemonic techniques successfully used in the young population. The results were negative at first, which led us to look into the cognitive changes encountered with aging. (I was determined to prove that you can teach an old human new tricks!) The main problem I noticed was psychological rejection of the mnemonic systems taught to memorize faces, names, and lists of words. Based on non-logical, even weird associations, these systems require the flexibility to play a new game and the ability to form mental images. We therefore designed a program to address the difficulties in a "preliminary training" to the mnemonic training: 1) relaxation training to relieve performance anxiety, which increases with age; 2) observation training to rekindle the ability to form mental images, which diminishes with age; and 3) extension of the training to compensate for the slowing down of the brain metabolism that comes with aging. The most successful package proved to be a pre-training combination of visual and verbal skills labeled "imagery + judgment," along with a lengthened mnemonic-training period. (Making a judgment mobilizes organizational skills and involves the person both intellectually and emotionally.) The courses have been taught by the same instructor (myself) for two hours per day, two weeks in a row, more or less continuously ever since.

Studies are still going on,[1] in the hope of understanding more how various memory-enhancement strategies work and explain-

---

[1] Our grant for these studies, financed by the National Institute of Mental Health, was renewed in 1991 for ten more years.

ing individual variations. The goal is to adapt the training to the individual's needs, and thus to increase the efficacy of the training, with obvious benefits to the individual and the community. Changes in our society may imply more and more job recycling; meanwhile, life expectancy has increased to the point of swelling the ranks of senior citizens. But one does not learn in the same way at all the stages of life. It is my belief that the more strategies are used in combination—and the more concrete the strategies are—the better at any age.

I am often asked whether I practice the strategies I teach, and I must confess "Yes, I do!" because they work, and give me a pleasant feeling of control. And when I happen to forget something, I understand why. Understanding a mechanism is reassuring, which in itself is important. Yet understanding is only the beginning. Everybody agrees that "An ounce of prevention is worth a pound of cure," but few people apply this prescription to memory. Prevention is the key to organization and recall. The sooner one learns principles of good retention, the better. The success of any training lies in reviewing and using efficient strategies. Only practice will improve your memory. And it will.

INTRODUCTION: THE PERSISTENCE OF MEMORY

The idea that every experience, every image is recorded in our memory, is a myth that Israel Rosenfield destroys in his book *The Invention of Memory: a New View of the Brain*. From Plato to the founders of the theory of localization of memory in the brain, established in the 19th century, down to Freud, the concept of "permanent memory" has clouded the fact that memory, serving the present, is pragmatic and could not function without its ally: forgetting. Acknowledging that memories are fragmentary, Freud studied the ways in which dreams and emotional states determine memories. He was the first to describe the function of the limbic system, nowadays widely recognized to "fix" memories, thus proving that not everything is registered equally, nor kept untouched.

Another way of demystifying memory is simply to look at how differently people remember the same experience. The distortion factor has been picked up humorously by Maurice Chevalier in the song *I Remember It Well; his* recollection of that special night turns out to be quite different from *hers.* In the visual arts, Salvador Dali's famous and insightful surrealistic painting, *The Persistence of Memory,* depicts clocks in recognizable but distorted form, as if partially melted.

Indeed, new studies suggest that one's memories are continually being altered, transformed, distorted. Every time one remembers something, one tampers with the memory trace, adding to it some present association or weakening part of it by neglecting to recall it. Elizabeth Loftus, a specialist in eyewitness testimony, explains that memory traces do not remain intact, but undergo changes as we literally construct and reconstruct memories each time we recall them. Memories, like the self, are subjective and in constant flux.

Memory is a complex mental process that can be understood—and should be, if we are to make the most of it. Paradoxically, forgetting is essential to memory function: Selective attention could not exist without it; while remembering one thing, one necessarily pushes aside others. One does not usually complain about forgetting useless material. Many people with extraordinary memories are not happier, because their minds are cluttered with irrelevant details they wish they could forget! In normal memory function there is a healthy balance.

Modern research proves that asking the right questions leads to the right answers. Asking questions and looking for answers are the first steps towards action. I have grouped about 100 questions in a natural sequence, from general to specific, with a last section consisting of new, open questions: 1) Demystifying Memory; 2) Focusing Attention; 3) Mnemonics: Tricks for Recall;

4) Medical Issues; and 5) Reflections on Memory. After each question, explanations are given, followed by suggestions whenever possible. The question-and-answer format has the big advantage of demonstrating memorization strategies at work in numerous different contexts, as is the case in everyday living. This gives rise to a repetition effect: As you proceed throughout the book you may begin to experience a sense of *deja vu*—proof, if you think about it, that you are remembering what you've read in other sections and are assimilating the principles of good retention. In addition, you will be learning an assortment of techniques to help you recall all kinds of information.

The first question in your mind may be: What stuff are memories made of? The answer is very interesting: They are made of feelings, moods, thoughts, words involving the senses, the emotions, the imagination, and the intellect. Indeed, memory involves the whole self. By acting on each mode, you can make the most of your memory.

The French literary master La Rochefoucault noted that "everyone complains about his memory and nobody complains about his judgment." Amusing as this piece of wisdom may be, the real irony lies in new research findings: Judgment, *whether good or bad*, is an adjunct to memory. Rather than being in opposition to one another, memory and judgment are complementary, since judgment relies on memory, which is itself consolidated by judgment.

Making comments to yourself or others—using judgment—is part of the panoply of mental strategies that enhance memory. To give you an idea of what mental strategies are, let me start by asking YOU one question that will probe your current memory skills: What do you do, or fail to do, in order to help your memory?

Do You Use Recall Strategies? Which Ones?

This general question seems difficult to those who are not

familiar with recall strategies, notes John Harris from Cambridge University in England, in a study on the methods people use for remembering. I thought you would like to answer a slightly modified version of his questionnaire and, in so doing, discover how much you participate in the recall process. At the end we will return to the conclusions of this study.

Do You Use:

1) lists to run your errands?
2) first-letter mnemonics (such as "HOMES," to recall the five Great Lakes of the United States)?
3) a diary?
4) rhymes or riddles (such as "Thirty days hath September, April, June, and November . . . ")?
5) the "Loci method," to remember long lists of items in order?
6) mental retracing of sequences of events or actions to reconstitute what happened or to find a lost object?
7) a timer, alarm clock, or watch—first only to wake up, then to remember something else like shutting off the sprinklers, removing the clothes from the dryer, etc.?
8) the "Peg method" of recalling numbers by associating them with words or letters?
9) a mnemonic trick to associate names and faces?
10) recitation of the alphabet to jog recall of a name?
11) an agenda and a calendar? Specify how.
12) calling on someone to remind you of something?
13) visual cues posted in prominent places like the refrigerator door?
14) various tricks such as making a knot in your handkerchief?
15) other strategies to record information? Explain.
16) other strategies to help recall? Explain.

Notice that there are two kinds of memory aids: "exterior" or mechanical aids, and "interior" or mental-strategy aids. These can be used at the time of recording or at the time of recall, or both.

Well, then, what do you do to help your memory? Not much? Now compare yourself to the average person.

What comes out of Harris's study of interviews of groups of students whose average age was 21 and adults from 23 to 67 years old is that "interior," mental strategies are seldom used; among those that *are* used, one finds mostly *recall* strategies such as "retrace events" and "use the alphabet" to recall a name. *Recording* strategies are rarely mentioned. The upshot: Most people fail to participate fully in the memory process.

One fact is clear: It is infinitely easier to remember something if a cue is planted at the time of recording. In this book, you will learn the principles of **observation training** (learning to capture details and differences), the **pause** (becoming aware of what you are doing), **relaxation** (removing anxiety and tension to become more receptive), **selective attention** (defining what you want to remember, why, and for how long), **image-association** (recording information in the visual mode as if your mind were a camera planting visual cues between different elements), and **verbal elaboration** (making comments, both intellectual and emotional, on the subject).

I hope that you will soon be convinced of the efficacy of the mental strategies you are about to learn, and that you will start using them regularly. They constitute a method easy to integrate into your everyday life.

DEMYSTIFYING MEMORY

Before we proceed to specific strategies for improving attention and retention, let us consider a number of questions that people commonly ask about how memory works.

1. What is "memory"?

No single definition can fully cover the scope of the subject. Therefore, a few have to be analyzed and combined, because they are complementary. Webster reads as follows: "1(a): The power or process of reproducing or recalling what has been learned or retained especially through associative mechanisms. (b): the store of things learned and retained . . ."

Memory is a mental process that entails three main operations: **recording, storage,** and **recall.** The main strategy at work seems to be association. These definitions refer only to human memory, hence the emphasis on psychological mechanisms. Author Alexander Chase describes it as a selective, subjective operation of the mind: "Memory is the thing you forget with." His paradoxical statement points toward the role will and consciousness play in the selection of memories to store for the longer or shorter term.

Forgetting is part of the memory mechanism, because it allows concentration on one subject at a time. When you are immersed in your work, you choose to forget temporarily, and hence to put aside all other matters. The example of the astrophysicist able to travel to distant stars, yet forever getting lost at the airport, speaks for itself. Everyone is more or less aware of his/her system of priorities. That is why it is good to ask ourselves which are the areas of our weakest interest. If you don't like numbers, you will avoid them and not even try to retain them, preferring to delegate the task to someone else.

Memory involves the whole brain, but it is first of all a biological phenomenon with its roots in the senses. There are several types of memories: visual, verbal, olfactory, tactile, kinesthetic, etc. In the animal world we find a genetic memory that determines the migration of whales, birds, and fish and the herd-instinct behavior of bees, ants, and cattle. The human variant is infinitely more complex, a reflection of a brain whose neuronal activity has the ability to sift, choose, cultivate, and eliminate memories. This sifting, whether conscious or unconscious, occurs through a web of emotions sometimes so painful that, as the poet Matthew Arnold said, "We forget because we must. And not because we will." Victims seldom remember their assailants, nor can they relate the details of the traumatic ordeal. Psychoanalysis tries to resuscitate these "repressed" memories.

2. Are there different types of memory?

This question concerns only the psychological aspect of human memory, memory in general having been addressed in the preceding question. It is not a simple matter, but I will try to explain it without splitting too many hairs. Human memory is often apprehended as a single mechanism, but in fact there are two distinct manifestations of memory corresponding to different mental processes: *voluntary* or *involuntary*. The sight of a photograph or the sound of a voice may trigger an involuntary memory if the sensation comes by surprise, or a voluntary one if one chooses to search for it. Dwelling on a sensation allows the passage from involuntary to voluntary recall.

A further distinction: Although memory and perception cannot be disassociated, one can speak of *visual* vs. *verbal* (that is, auditory) memory. About 60 percent of the population is predominantly visual. These people visualize easily places, objects, faces, the pages of a newspaper. The others seem to better remember sounds or words, and the associations that come to their mind are often rhymes or puns.

Whether it be voluntary or involuntary, visual or verbal, memory exists within the frame of time: It is up to us to decide what is worth remembering for an hour, a day, or years to come. The necessities of life (studies, work, or other priorities) guide us in this continual choice, and so do our personal interests. Memory adapts to our needs. But we often fail to notice that these needs change with the circumstances. We remember people's names when we deal with them, and we lose this aptitude if we lead isolated lives, as is the case with retirement and many solitary types of work. Memory being essentially pragmatic, it relies on different kinds of mechanisms depending on whether the information is to be used right away or later on.

Immediate perceptual memory is a reflex memory in which an impression is immediately replaced by a new one, as is the case in typing. As soon as a letter is typed it is forgotten so that one can attend to the next. Here, forgetting one letter and focusing on another happen quasi-simultaneously. Another example is the reading of words on a page. These memory traces do not need to be consolidated or stored, since they are used immediately. Bypassing consciousness, they also unburden it.

Short-term memory is a working memory capable, according to psychologists' definition, of recording seven elements for a maximum of thirty seconds. It is used when looking up and then immediately dialing a phone number. In case this is not possible—for instance when you cannot write it down—you must keep repeating the number until it is used. Should an interruption occur, the number vanishes because it had not been registered so as to be recalled later. This is normal, for these short-term memory traces are made by less-complex mechanisms than are long-term memory traces. They are shallower and more short-lived, disappearing almost as soon as they have appeared as if they had been etched on a magic slate. Without this working memory, many actions would be slowed down by traffic jams of old information. Short-term memory makes it possible to dispatch data that becomes irrelevant as soon as it is used. Its very fragility is functional; for it prompts us to use it as soon as possible. Note that in scientific jargon this term does not refer to what people mean by recent memories (hours, days) as opposed to older memories (months, years). In fact such "mid-term" memories properly belong to the domain of long-term memory; scientifically speaking, the term "mid-term memory" does not exist.

Long-term memory must by definition leave a more or less long-term memory trace, on the order of a few minutes, days, or years. In order to do so, it relies on more-complex information-processing mechanisms located on several levels: sensory, emotional, and intellectual. There are only two types of recording processes: one without, and one with, **depth of processing.**

"Sweeping" memory, the shortest of all long-term memories, involves little depth of processing. Air-traffic controllers develop this faculty, which allows them to focus on a spot on the screen for a few minutes until the plane has landed, then forget it, replacing it with another.

When information is to be used in the near future, as is the case for examinations, presentations, or a specific message like an address or a reminder to the baker to hold a cake for you, intensive repetition helps maintain information up front. But mechanical repetition is only a short-term tool; it does not guarantee long-term recall, which is why cramming for examinations is a poor learning strategy. To consolidate a memory trace for long-term retention, more depth of processing is needed—a goal, for example, as well as time to think, integrate, and review information. Long-term memory relies on observation, analysis, and judgment. This is referred to as the process of **elaboration.**

Any judgment involves affect, or emotion. If I ask you right off the bat to remember your high-school or/and university teachers, you may be surprised to find there are so few! You can probably count them on the fingers of one hand. Those you do recall after so many years are those you admired, loved, feared, or hated.

Memory traces were not born equal: Each has been sifted and recorded differently. Strong emotions act as seals, leaving a superior memory trace. One can improve the **recording** of memories by becoming aware of feelings, and by developing better observation skills leading to comments (to yourself or to others) that tap into both intellect and emotion. In this light, why you remember certain details becomes clearer: For instance, I remember a substitute math teacher I had in high school partly because she was booed, partly because of her comical appearance: a round, small, ageless woman, carrying large T-squares and rigged out in a black floppy hat, with shoes cut around huge bunions. I can visualize her clearly although I cannot recall her name—which proves the superiority of visual memory. One can improve **recall** by learning to plant **cues** using files or categories. For example, if I open my "comic" file, other teachers, other situations appear on the screen of my mind. It is amusing to follow these associations as far as possible.

3. Where is memory located in the brain?

Since the theory of functional localization was born from Broca's studies in the 19th century, it has been acknowledged that memory is diffuse—that is, located in different parts of the brain, according to whether it is related to a sensation or an emotion. The anatomic supports of memory include the cortex, divided into different zones corresponding to the different senses and motor functions; the limbic system; and the cerebellum. But most of the neurophysiological activity that constitutes memory takes place in the hippocampus, found in the temporal lobes on either side of the brain. If one of the lobes is injured, memory, although disrupted, can still function. But if both are damaged, the capacity for recording and recalling information on a voluntary basis is destroyed. This may be caused by physical injuries of the temporal lobes or by neurochemical deficits, as is the case in degenerative diseases affecting memory such as Alzheimer's disease.

4. Is there a chemistry of memory?

Certainly! Memory's work coincides with the activity of nerve cells, or **neurons,** which communicate among themselves in the brain. The messengers are specialized molecules (called neurotransmitters) such as acetylcholine, which is found in quantity in the hippocampus. A deficit in acetylcholine is like running out of gas. Learning processes cannot take place; only involuntary memory is accessible, through sensation. This is the plight of the amnesiac patient, unable to remember while in his house the word "snow," which miraculously comes to him as he touches it, only to disappear again once he returns indoors.

The slowing of metabolism that parallels aging is a well-known and important neurochemical change. The body's metabolic processes involve the combustion of glucose or fats to produce energy, some of which is used to manufacture acetylcholine in the brain. With normal aging, the production of acetylcholine, although somewhat diminished, is sufficient to guarantee good mental function. One of the probable consequences of reduced amounts of acetylcholine and other neurotransmitters is the slowing down of mental functions affecting memory; one may notice a brief delay of response to a stimulus, both at the time of observation and recording and at the time of recall. To function better as you get older, it is wise to become more patient with yourself: It is only a matter of a few seconds difference, but if you let the delay get to you, it will make matters worse. To compensate, you can learn strategies that facilitate and speed recall, thus making it possible to function well, at least up to a certain age, provided you are in good health.

5. How does memory develop throughout the life span?

Since memory is a function but also a skill, it implies development, which can clearly be observed from childhood to old age. As we have seen, it involves the senses, emotions, the intellect, the personality, the whole self, which takes a lifetime to develop! The young child learns through perception and slowly integrates cognitive skills, such as language and imagery, that develop simultaneously. She needs to establish frames of reference in order to remember.

Recognition is the first type of memory to appear. At this stage the child is passive and merely identifies stimuli. As language develops, descriptive skills are honed, but they are activated only by social interaction play and schooling. Spontaneous strategies to recall information—that is, active intervention—

are late to develop (age 9–10).

The years of adolescence are most important in the development of learning strategies, and we should make the most of them. Memory development peaks with cognitive development. Memory is better in adults because after they have reached the height of their cognitive skills, they have developed strategies in tune with the demands of their environment: The number of things we need to remember in order to function in everyday life is amazing. As long as the need is there, we find a way (or strategy) to make sure we do not forget. By learning better-than-average, foolproof strategies, we can increase our efficiency at any age. As a matter of fact, the older we get the more we need strategies to compensate for decline of certain functions.

True, memory declines slightly with age, but as among children, there are many individual differences. Adults are the most homogeneous population. However, an interesting study comparing chessplaying children with adult non-chessplayers showed that these children remembered chessboard positions better than adults because they were meaningful and familiar to them. Thus the concepts of meaning and practice are crucial to memory at any age, in any context.

Children and older people share many common difficulties that explain their reduced memory performance:

- shorter attention span
- lack of awareness
- lack of spontaneous organization
- difficulty in focusing and selecting the most important elements
- passivity: they fail to act for their own mnemonic good
- difficulty forming mental pictures
- reduced energy for making associations related to the information to be remembered
- limited goal setting

Danielle C. Lapp

The main difference seems to be that young children remember recent acquisitions better, and older people older ones (because they are processing new material less efficiently). But come to think of it, it is still something they have in common: for different reasons—lack of development of cognitive skills or reduction of those skills—they do not record information efficiently.

Thus, memory function seems to form a loop throughout the life cycle. Let us make the most of it at any age by learning how to help it with the practice of mental strategies.

6. How does children's memory develop?

Although we are not always aware of recording information, mental strategies have taken place voluntarily or involuntarily whenever we remember. At first the young child is passive and learns through perception by responding to stimuli, which she identifies as objects or people at around 3 months of age. At first, the baby smiles at everyone. Only at around 6 months can she differentiate her parents from strangers, and she starts crying at unfamiliar faces. At around one year, she utters her first word, and the following months show a slow progress in speech development. By two the child may have 37 words minimum in her repertory. (There are great individual references—from 6 to 126 words). Interestingly mental imagery does not precede, but develops simultaneously with, language acquisition. It is clear that the ability to visualize is linked to knowledge of reality. The young child has to get acquainted with the world first in order to be able to recreate it in the form of mental pictures.

"Recognition" memory—a passive kind of memory—precedes active recall, which implies conscious participation. *The preschooler, like the infant, does not use spontaneous strategies* to recall, as she is just sorting out the relationships between past, present, and future. Few 6-year-olds do something specific to remember, whereas 9-year-olds do. By then the child has learned that she

9

can control recall by doing something such as placing her skates next to her school bag. It is only in adolescence that children use strategies systematicall; the cognitive functions have matured, and they can use them all. Whether children possess limited processing resources or do not know how to use them is a theoretical question. The fact is that only older children use a cue as a starting point for an extensive memory search. By doing so, they are showing themselves to be actively involved in the process of recording and recalling information. They have gained flexibility in using what they have learned, which was lacking in younger children.

All these remarks stem from tests given within contexts devoid of personal motivation. Empirical studies monitored by diaries show that children can organize and use strategies efficiently at an earlier age for specific limited tasks necessary to their social interactions. This opens the door to fostering the teaching and learning of strategies in every context. Parents and teachers can motivate and stimulate the child at any age, in specific ways that develop their memory. Memory development can be helped at school and at home by teaching mental strategies and rehearsing them regularly. Cross cultural studies have shown that school helps the onset of mental strategies by repeatedly placing demands on children to perform memory tasks.

Most studies show that training in the use of recall strategies does produce a change in development of children's faculties. Stages of maturity do exist, but they are flexible. As the child matures, she uses her growing knowledge to establish elaborate, meaningful relations with respect to information, and as a consequence, remembers more accurately.

7. What are the major causes of memory problems at any age?

Except for the pathological cases we shall discuss later on, the main causes of memory problems are psychological in nature. Among the young, as among the not-so-young, memory lapses occur in very specific contexts where anxiety interferes with attention: stage fright, examinations, public speaking, fatigue or nervous exhaustion, stress, personal problems. Children who live in difficult family circumstances often have difficulties concentrating on their schoolwork. People suffering from stress and overwork often complain about forgetting many things, and so do retired people who, watching their memories dwindle, despair because they do not realize that something can be done about it.

Anxiety and depression are the two major causes of memory problems at any age. They monopolize attention so that it is impossible to concentrate on anything else. In these extreme emotional states a person does not notice the exterior world, but instead turns inwards and fails to record information the way he/she does when the mind is free to attend. The thought processes are occupied only with negative thoughts, and there is no room for other thoughts that could help jog the memory. In order to remember, you must be able to think or at least to perceive through the senses, thus triggering involuntary memory. Yet depressed people notice and remember only depressing things that reflect their condition. This is natural, since recall is triggered by associations. In an anxious state one worry brings about another, in a chain of despair. The malaise is worsened by mental ruminations such as: "I should be able to remember the name of this plant in my living room." One draws a terrible blank and self-blame ensues.

This vicious circle can only be interrupted by changing the subject or by relaxing. Whenever anxiety arises, tell yourself: "I'm going to have to calm down and pay double attention if I am to remember this." Knowing that anxiety impedes memory function helps stop people from feeling guilty. But even better, the following simple breathing exercises restore the inner peace in a few seconds:

- Imagine that you are at the seashore, watching the waves on a beautiful summer morning. Let yourself be transported by the brisk air and iodine smell. Projecting sensory awareness will help you relax.

- Breathe deeply and gradually through your nose, visualizing a wave building up as you inhale, then rolling back and dissolving on the shore as you exhale.

- Listen to the sound of the waves as you continue to inhale and exhale deeply, gradually, at a regular pace.

- Ride the waves until you feel like yawning—a sure sign of relaxation.

Another strategy: When a difficult question arises, ignore it or dodge it, delaying your answer by continuing to talk about the subject. This cuts anxiety short and lets you regain control of the conversation. It also buys more time for the memory to return. Recall is rarely instantaneous, and the more obstacles, the more time it takes your internal scanner to access information. With age, anxiety increases because of the real delay in response that accompanies the slowing down of metabolism. An older person may become impatient, start worrying, and finally blame him/herself without realizing he/she is making matters worse. There is a paradox with respect to word recall: The harder you try to force it from "the tip of your tongue," the longer it will take to resurface. The reason is that as you attempt to speed up recall, you get nervous and create the very anxiety that compounds the problem. Only by shifting to another subject can you let the scanner do its work at its own rhythm. It is wise to accept the slower pace without lamenting (often idealized!) bygone days. You can become an expert at hiding these lapses by using a synonym or beating around the bush making interesting remarks. It is relaxing to dwell on what you are saying rather than think about what you are going to say next.

Above all, minimize the importance of such incidents: They do not mean trouble. Giving yourself time and means to vanquish anxiety is the key to memory control at any age, but in particular as you get older and the frequency of delays increases. Integrate relaxation into your mental hygiene.

There are, of course, circumstances in which only time and a change of situation may restore the peace of mind necessary to concentrate. Those who are depressed by the death of a loved one or the loss of a job should take it in stride and postpone challenging their memories to a date when they have overcome their temporary difficulties. In such a state of mind, forgetting is common and inevitable, and learning capacity is at an all-time low. First, depression must be lifted, liberating the mind from its paralyzing obsessional thoughts. When you are again ready to pay attention to the world around you, your memory will come back on its own.

8. Do grief and sorrow interfere with memory?

Yes, as I have just said. Memory troubles are common in people suffering from grief. Since all their thoughts converge on their sorrow, there is not enough energy to concentrate on anything else. As this condition improves, there comes a renewed interest in other subjects. Sometimes one manages for a while to distract grieving individuals, but this does not mean they are healed. They often tend to throw themselves into some kind of activity to drown their sorrows, but they are still not able to attend to the present, which is why they forget so much in their daily affairs. For the grief-stricken, coarse visual and auditory reminders such as stickers and timers are a must! They should not hesitate to use them.

In some extreme cases, attention difficulties are such that it is inadvisable to drive a car. I remember having taken a sharp left turn into the left lane of a two-way street as I was driving back from the clinic where my first husband had just been told he had to have bypass surgery. In my agitated state of mind, I found it excruciatingly difficult to pay attention to the road. This kind of reaction must be common, because, sometime later, the surgeon insisted so much that someone drive me home after he informed me of my husband's death. One must acknowledge that there are moments when it is dangerous to play superman.

9. In which situations is it difficult to sustain attention, making it impossible for memory to operate?

Under what conditions do memory lapses occur? Can we anticipate them? avoid them? Whether for recording or for recalling information, attention is indispensable. Alas! it is not always possible to sustain it. Attention is by nature fragile. Fortunately, many mechanisms have been devised to prevent catastrophic consequences—for instance, when writing a check, the reason you must write the sum in ciphers and again in letters is that the repetition forces you to pay attention in order to make them coincide. In case they do not (owing to your distraction), the check is void. Another example: Pilots have a checklist for takeoff and landing procedures so that they do not skip any important steps. They use visual reminders such as placing the flight plan on the door handle of the plane so that they will remember to call the flight controllers upon landing at a remote airport.

In general, you can anticipate attention problems and prevent the consequences mentioned above. But in order to do so, you must be able to identify the situations in which your attention is most vulnerable, as itemized in the following list:

- when you are rushed
- when you are under stress
- when you are momentarily distracted
- when you are interrupted

- when you digress
- when emotions are overwhelming (excitement, euphoria, rage)
- when you are absorbed in a task or deep in thought
- when you are tired or drowsy (overworked, under the influence of drugs or alcohol)
- when in familiar surroundings (because your guard is down)
- when you are operating "on autopilot" (habitual or "automatic gestures")
- when you cannot make sense of information

Beware of all these situations: You will have to modify them and be extra-careful in order to avoid forgetting something. Should it happen, you will at least know why: Your mind was not on what you were doing! Once and for all you will be able to differentiate between *attention* problems vs. *retention* problems. As William James wrote: "An object *once attended to* will remain in memory, whereas one inattentively allowed to pass will leave no traces."

10. How do surroundings, moods, and emotions influence memory?

In different ways. Studies have shown that a person remembers better when placed in the same conditions (whether a place or a mood) as those in which the learning occurred. Thus, a group of subjects who had learned a list of words under water remembered a greater number of them immersed in this element than in a classroom test. When one is "blue," all the memories that spring back to consciousness are tinted with melancholy. In the vicious circle of depression all associations are negative, matching the mood of the moment. It always proves difficult to break this chain of negative associations. However, it is possible to do it by modifying the mood with the help of music, reading, movies, TV, work, travel, friendship.

Emotions play a complex role, both positive and negative, in memory function. They are so powerful that they can effectively seal the memory trace, protecting it from the ravages of forgetfulness. This is their positive effect: We remember mostly, and for longer, what moves and touches our souls. For instance, among my wedding memories, strong emotions and impressions prevail over guests, place, and menu. I remember the luminous light of Napa Valley, so similar to my native Provence in France, its scents, the ideal temperature of this beautiful spring day. Then I visualize the balcony of our room overlooking the splendid view of the valley, above which colorful hot air balloons floated gaily, rising towards the hills. A wave of emotions lifts me up, bringing me many details of the ceremony, the reception, the meal. Mostly positive scenes, but negative details, too, like that beautiful cake covered with green almond paste—when I had ordered it white! Come to think of it, it was probably prettier this way, or in any case, more original. I did not make an issue out of it at the time, and I have forgotten whatever was not meaningful to me. But I will never forget a certain few symbolic details coated with emotion. And aren't these all that matter? Friends and pictures can complete the rest; since memory is subjective, everyone will remember something else.

The negative side of emotions is that they interfere with attention, as seen above. When strong emotions occur, they sweep and monopolize attention, making it impossible to attend to anything else. When angry or elated, we are not very likely to be observant. One must accept this fact. However, provided we remember what we care about, this should be more than enough.

11. Can I gain control over my memory?

Yes, more than you think. It is true that we record many things at a subliminal level, and that these memories can be activated subconsciously, as is the case with certain advertisements employing eroticism. Traces drenched in emotion remain vivid in our memory, and we do not control them. Most of the time, involuntary memory percolates up spontaneously, although we can increase the number of episodes of recall by becoming more observant. If I notice more things, I have a greater chance of recapturing multiple associations. If I use more than one sense—for example, touch and taste in addition to sight and hearing—I will trigger more memories. In this instance involuntary memory merges with voluntary memory—the one we can act upon. To do so, we must move from a passive to an active state, stop counting on automatic processes, and shift to manual—that is, conscious control. (This is particularly recommended for older people whose "spontaneous organizational reflexes" are on the decline.) Driving your memory, like driving a car, is part reflex, part awareness, part strategy, part practice. It is in your power to determine what you wish to remember for the shorter or longer term, and act accordingly.

Each time you remember a detail, it is because you have done something special: initiated a **pause** to fix your attention on what has interested you, and also probably formulated a **mental comment.** The more you become aware of memory processes, the more you will be able to control them. In deciding to make an effort to remember a store so that I can tell a friend about it, I define a goal in time and space. I give myself the motivation to fix important details such as name of the store, the street, interesting items, prices. By anticipating the moment that I will communicate my message to my friend, and by imagining her reaction to it, I record an emotion, which will strengthen the memory trace. If I get into the habit of taking mental pictures of my surroundings, recording them in a visual mode and formulating comments, I participate in the memory process. There exist many "mental strategies" that guarantee recording and recall superior to the mediocre average. You can isolate the principles behind efficient action: steps like anticipating forgetfulness; pausing to channel attention, thus giving yourself time to think; grouping in categories; concretizing abstract concepts; looking for meaning; making **image-associations** (associating one visualized image with another, so that the thought of one induces recall of the other) and **verbal comments.** It is up to you to learn these strategies and practice them in context.

12. Is memory, like beauty, a gift?

To the extent that the notion of "gift" implies "inheritance and passivity," memory is not a gift but rather *a skill,* one that depends on applying appropriate strategies in various contexts. Nobody remembers "everything" in the same way. Because memory is subjective, each person chooses to remember what interests him/her. Thus, some have a memory for numbers, others for names, still others for places, etc. If gift there be, it is the basic capacity to focus on one subject. A casual observer notices that certain children are more attentive than others. Their curiosity seems above average, and they show more interest in the world around them. Some have a facility to learn by rote, but forget fast. Few are those, however, who challenge their memory just for fun as do *mnemonists,* whose memories seem extraordinary. What do these pros do differently from you and me? One of them, Jerry Lucas, says his astounding memory for the spelling of difficult words goes back to the long car trips he took with his parents when still a young boy: As soon as he knew how, he started reading the billboards for the simple reason that he got bored and had to find a distraction. To pass the time he turned the exercise into a game, and with this goal in mind, he had devised a strategy. He would read and analyze words, spelling and visualizing each letter, *forwards and backwards*! To everyone's amazement this child could spell a word he had "studied" in *both* directions. As this example shows, a combination of motivation, concentration, and practical organization (or strategy) produces spectacular results. Some mnemonists, resorting to clusters of image-associations they made thirty years ago, can recall lists of words given to them at that time. These extraordinary memories are much more selective than ordinary ones, and that is partly why they impress us so. Their specialization goes beyond reason—and sometimes beyond intelligence! The "idiot savant" remembers many useless details.

Memory is more egalitarian than you may think, since everyone has the ability to remember what interests him/her. The challenge is to learn how to maintain interest in everyday things. When motivation changes, as is the case at different stages of life, practice decreases or ceases. What is the use of remembering a quotation once you no longer need to impress anyone by repeating it? Both social environment and frame of mind strongly determine the motivation to act.

In the final analysis, it does not matter whether memory is a gift or not, for gifts must be cultivated or they go to seed. In order to protect one's beauty one must take good care of it. Just as with a musical gift, one must develop one's memory through constant practice, or it will weaken. Telling yourself that memory is a gift may lead, counterproductively, to abdication of your responsibility for developing it. Any gift is relative; it is work, practice, and discipline that set virtuosi apart from the rest of us. Those good at rote learning favor it; others who learn foreign languages with ease cultivate that skill instead. Virtually everyone possesses an adequate memory, which needs only to be developed in order to become "exceptional" in the context of one's life. Analyze the strategies you use successfully in the areas you excel in, and transfer them to others. If you remember statistics easily, you can remember other numbers, too, provided you are motivated. Without adequate motivation you will not make enough of an effort, and you will need to use a mnemonic to remember numbers.

Rather than a gift, *memory is a skill.* Studies on intelligence suggest that in everyday life one only uses 10 percent of the potential of the brain. Specific training allows us to do better: British researchers have found that almost anyone can be trained to take the IQ test, and that improvement can be measured across all levels of intelligence. While there is always much debate about such findings, what is certain is that the limits of human possibilities are far from being reached. We can "experiment" on ourselves, using strategies that have proven their worth. Not everyone succeeds as well with the same method. Individual differences exist at every age and every IQ level.

13. Are memory and intelligence related?

Yes and no! When speaking about memory in general, one must answer yes. In his book *Memory and the Brain: The Biology of Learning,* which describes the anatomic, chemical, and physiological sources of memory in the animal world, Georges Chapouthier concludes: "One sees emerging the image of a memory made of successive stages corresponding to the complexity of the brain, which explains the lesser capacities of species other than the human." In man the problem is more complex, as revealed by studies on exceptional memories. Examples of idiots savants are common in the literature; the mnemonic systems they use with awesome mastery to memorize telephone books, or to calculate with lightning speed the day of the week on which any date you provide will fall, can improve the performance of subjects of different levels of intelligence. In the more intelligent subject, when this "artificial memory" is added to the spontaneous organization already there, spectacular results ensue, in many different areas. This is very different from the narrowly specific performance of the idiot savant who may, perhaps, excel at recalling numbers—but only at that, to the exclusion of almost every other mental activity. In brief, intelligence allows a person to think of and apply recall systems in *mutiple* contexts. However, it is human to want to specialize in those areas that interest us. This selective focusing of attention on the part of some highly intelligent people gives rise to the syndrome of the "absent-minded professor," who cares and notices only what is related to his work. His memory is not defective, merely overspecialized and narrowly focused.

14. Are memory and personality related?

On personality tests measuring intuition, obsessive-compulsive behavior, and extroversion, it is difficult to read anything precise. The attention of obsessive people is more rigid, less available but more intense, explains David Shapiro in his book *Neurotic Styles.* He gives the example of workaholics who live for their work, which has become a fixation they cannot drop or stay away from. At the opposite end of the spectrum is the hysteric type, easily dominated by his/her sensations and feelings and therefore more vulnerable to distractions and interferences. In both cases attention is reduced. Fortunately people's personalities are usually a mix of several types, albeit with a definite emphasis on one or another.

In the empirical realm of everyday life, however, one notices differences, especially concerning the ability to learn. People who are easily distracted, dreamy types poorly rooted in reality forget practical information they consider unimportant. The memory potential is there, but is constrained by the focusing of their attention only upon their priorities. Thus they will forget their coat or where they parked their car, but not a single detail of something they really care about. At its core, this is an attention deficit, not a retention deficit: If nothing is recorded, there is nothing to recall. At fault is not memory, but rather the personality determining what is worth remembering. Because personality characteristics get accentuated with age, absent-minded people have a tendency to become even more vague, less precise, less functional as they grow older. They depend more and more on others.

Personality also plays a role in the capacity to *improve* your memory at any age. In classes composed of subjects over 55 years old, which I have taught countless times in conjunction with the Stanford University School of Medicine, I have found that not everyone improves in the same way. Those who succeed best seem to have a direction to their lives. They set goals and work toward them. They are more active. They assume responsibility for their improvement and are less likely than others to blame external factors such as age or loss of nerve cells. They believe that it is up to them to learn the mnemonic systems that have proven so effective for others (a fact they accept as true, rather than challenge it in the name of logic—for most mnemonic methods are based on non-logical associations.) If we accept full responsibility for learning, we learn better. At any age, excellent students study first for themselves, then to please teachers or parents.

The second personality trait associated with learning ability is an open mind, even a taste for risk and adventure. The person who is ready to accept new ideas, to make new experiences, to venture into the unknown without worrying about possible consequences, will naturally be willing to try new mental strategies. The results are spectacular and speak for themselves: If you just try it, you'll learn to like it!

Then there are the anxious personalities, so preoccupied with their doubts and insecurities that they cannot attend to new material to be learned, which they often, more or less consciously, question *a priori*. Anxious people do not dare try new things, often donning the mask of skepticism to justify the fact that they are less open to new learning: for instance, a Mrs. S., who kept on interrupting the class to explain why she could not visualize and why this could not work for her. Instead of trying the strategies, she discussed them and fought them. Another flatly refused to participate in the study because she wanted guarantees that this type of training would not harm her. It was as if she feared a fast brainwashing! In fact, the great advantage of psychological interventions is precisely that there are no side effects to worry about, as is the case with drug studies.

Another scenario: the interior monologue of the individual who fears criticism. Anxiety jails the personality by inducing paralysis. The famous film critic Pauline Kael has written a sentence that is quite instructive in this regard: "An error in judgment is not fatal, but too much anxiety about judgment is." Indeed, while one can recover from an error in judgment (after all, people forget and life goes on), one does not easily recover from the fear of being judged, because it leads to silence and inaction. To renounce expressing your convictions is tantamount to abandoning ship; it is the end of creativity. Better to brace oneself for criticism and respond to it with an attitude reminiscent of President Franklin D. Roosevelt, who declared (was it to boost his courage?): "The only thing to fear is fear itself."

15. Is it possible to overload or underload memory? How are memories stored?

A difficult question, because it varies according to the individual and the circumstances. It seems evident that in times of stress or fatigue it is possible to overload your memory. When you study for hours at a time without taking a break or doing the least physical exercise, you tire your mind and saturate your memory. You notice that ideas are not so clear, and thinking is more difficult. This signals the need to stop, get some fresh air, and relax. Yes, you can saturate your memory for short or medium term, as happens with cramming, which consists of stockpiling as much information as possible in a minimum amount of time for immediate consumption.

That having been said, it is difficult to overload long-term memory, given its pragmatic nature—its auto-selection mechanism is constantly sifting information at both the conscious and unconscious levels. Only what is actually used remains fresh in mind.

The storage of memories is accomplished through a sophisticated system organized by "files" that are referred to at shorter or greater intervals in time, more or less frequently. Imagine thousands of such files: some *active,* that is, consulted regularly in everyday life; others *passive,* more rarely referred to, like those for foreign languages or faraway friends; and finally others that are *latent,* summoned up by means of a prompter.

The ability to forget temporarily and then, later, to retrieve memories through involuntary memory prevents the overload of long-term memory. Suggestion: By becoming more observant, you will trigger more involuntary associations, and you also will record more information, thereby leaving better cues. And if you learn to organize your thoughts at the time of recall by calling on "categories" (your file titles, such as "people," or "things," or "events"), the number of details you will remember will truly amaze you. For instance, to remember my first holidays in England (I was 16), first I am receptive to the strong images and feelings: The old town of Hastings on the English Channel, the mini-roses I used to snip in the garden every morning to put in my hair, the beach, the English courses, the meals, the people I met. These first images trigger others, but I can also consciously "extract" impressions from one category in particular, thus reviving numerous details: My "English course" file can be supplemented by exploring various other categories: students, teachers, curriculum, classroom. It is a game of multiple boxes within boxes, both useful and fun to play.

Ultimately, you can remember only in proportion to what you have recorded. If a file appears empty, chances are it has always been or it was emptied at some point in time. (Memories do get buried or eroded.) Instead of blaming your memory, congratulate it for what it brings back. The good news is that you can help it more than you thought.

By remaining mentally active, you will prevent the lack of stimulation that impoverishes memory. If you lose interest in everything and everybody, you inevitably register very little information. After retirement, for example, it is not always easy to find new goals and activities, especially if you are depressed. But this is precisely what your memory needs if it is to function. Without its being activated, it stops being used, and, as the saying goes: "Use it or lose it."

On the contrary, the more your memory is challenged, the better its health. As bones are strengthened by weight bearing exercises, so is memory strengthened by mental exercises. For instance, to better recall the third paragraph of the answer to this question, try visualizing three file folders of different symbolic colors: *blue* = active zone; *rust* = passive zone; *gray* = latent zone. Then find an example for each of these three types of memories. If you now visualize those examples sitting like files inside these folders, you will have recorded this organizational scheme on multiple levels: visual, intellectual, personal. Review it by talking to someone about it, or make comments to yourself on the subject. This way you will be sure you left a high-quality memory trace. Keep in mind that the more you review anything, the better: this keeps it afloat in the more accessible blue zone.

16. Are all memories recorded and preserved in the same way?

No, definitely not! Freud underlined the unconscious mechanisms that repress certain painful memories. Apart from these neurotic selections of the subconscious mind, there is the fact that we judge certain things to be more important to us than others, and this judgment determines how much we invest in the recording stage. However, the circumstances under which we record something play an important role. If you are tired, under stress, anxious, depressed, you will find it difficult to concentrate. Without concentrating, you cannot think straight. Motivation, which determines how much attention you give something, varies with mood and circumstances. Today, for instance, you may be especially interested in the news, perhaps because it seems more important or relevant; you listen better, you read the newspaper more carefully, you discuss unfolding developments at lunch with colleagues. All these steps leave a superior memory trace. Consequently this news will remain in your memory, whereas yesterday's may have already been washed away.

Motivation implies an emotional involvement, which strengthens the memory trace. You remember better what touches, shocks, moves you, whether the jolt is positive or negative. Voltaire said, "What touches the heart is engraved in memory." Search among your memories, and see if he was not right. The neutral is the enemy of memory because it neither evokes interest nor draws attention, and therefore triggers no reaction. Criminologists report that people best remember the most bizarre crimes, like those of Charlie Manson, who sent his LSD-crazed minions into the homes of Hollywood celebrities targeted for death, or of Jeffrey Daumer, the Milwaukee serial killer who cut his victims into little pieces, which he kept in his refrigerator to be eaten later.

Not only is information not equally recorded, but it is also not equally stored: Certain memories are retrieved more often than others, which reinforces their traces, connecting them to the new associations that brought them back. If you are interested in politics, you talk or think about it regularly, and references to past events, articles, or statements are constantly elicited. I can attest to the fact that in my work as a teacher, I remember first the examples I have quoted the most in the past, because they are more accessible in the blue zone of the present (see Question #13, this section), which I consult all the time. To renew my repertoire, I must make an extra effort and use notes, reviewing them several times before I integrate them into my lecture. The more one "rehearses" as if on stage, the better the memory trace. One remembers with ease, if with sadness, loved ones who have died but whose presence is there with us through once-shared photographs or objects.

A final point: Whenever you share with a loved one the memory of a past event, you notice that your recalled images and impressions differ quite a bit. Memory is subjective: Our personalities filter, interpret everything we are exposed to. You may be surprised upon being able to remember the wallpaper in your grandfather's living room. It is difficult to explain how the selection is made, but one thing is certain: It *is* made, and determines what will be recalled. Check with a friend, asking him/her to remember your first encounter. You will be astonished at how different your recollections are. This difference may highlight the nature of your friendship and your characters, as I found out. My friend X describes our first encounter in this way: "It was on the stairway at the university. You came to me and showed me where the next class was taking place." My recollection was that of another moment in class when our eyes met. I had found him timid and a bit lost. Since this impression proved right, it explains his recollection: I was helping him find his way, and he had been sensitive to my gesture or perhaps just amused by it. Definitely no!—memory traces are not all equal in importance nor intensity. Some disappear where others leave a strong mark, while still others bloom and expand because of multiple recalls.

Some dramatic events are remembered by everyone because they have been covered time and again by the media: for instance, the pictures of John F. Kennedy's assassination so often shown in documentaries and films. Everybody remembers what they were doing at the time they learned about it—in such extreme cases, where emotion plays a major role, personal details spring back. Personally, I recall that I was on a train to Germany when the news spread like gunpowder from car to car. Suddenly, my compartment was a beehive of strangers talking to one another in sorrow, turmoil, and total disbelief. I still can feel disillusionment tightening my throat, and the fear among the German passengers whom JFK had so recently reassured by saying "Ich bin ein Berliner."

In order to make a memory trace truly memorable, some extra focus involving emotion and intellect must be at work. Montaigne was right in stressing thinking strategies and rejecting rote scholastic learning in his *Essays*. Judgment and affect result in the elaboration of thoughts, which are then recorded on multiple levels. In any case, nowadays it proves more efficient to learn how to access information than try to remember all the details by heart. Let the computers do that!

17. Do memories remain intact, or are they altered with time?

In the preceding question I described the relative strength of recall in relation to what was happening at the moment of recording. Here I will look at the problem of the alteration of the memory trace *after* it has been recorded, which is as real as it is inevitable. Expert Elizabeth Loftus, who specializes in the testimony of eyewitnesses, puts it this way: "Even if we take in a reasonably accurate picture of some experience, it does not necessarily stay intact in memory. Another force is at work. The memory traces can actually undergo distortion. . . . Even in the most intelligent among us is memory thus malleable." That is probably why one speaks about idealizing the past. Unlike poets, most of us do not let our imagination go fishing for memories—even the unhappy ones. Rather, in our wish to look for pleasure and avoid suffering, we tend to rehearse the pleasant and leave aside the unpleasant. Not that the negative necessarily gets erased—we are sometimes surprised by involuntary memories that resuscitate painful moments, say, when we are transported by chance to the place where an accident happened—but one typically chooses voluntarily to remember happy and interesting moments, unless one has masochistic inclinations or is depressed; in the latter case, the repetition effect noted earlier can have adverse consequences, as the same gloomy scenarios run over and over in one's mind, taking root in the subconscious.

Each time you recall something, you add or leave out parts of the original memory. If the recollection occurs in the context of a conversation, the other party's questions or comments will put the accent on such or such a detail; if in the course of a personal reminiscence, selection of details is determined by the mood, the context, and the time allowed for recall. Stored once again, this memory is not exactly the same as it was. Consider the child's game of "telephone," in which the original message is distorted along the way by each person who repeats it, to the point of being unrecognizable.

We have seen that memory is made of many elements—emotional, sensory, intellectual, mood-, space-, and time-related—of which we are typically unaware. One filters all the stimuli according to one's personality, emphasizing one thing or another and capturing the signals of others selectively, through one's "cultural antennae." This selectivity can be a source of widely divergent interpretations and even outright misunderstandings. Thus, two people listen to a political speech and remember it quite differently.

As I listened to the news one day during the Persian Gulf War of 1990–91, a remark by an Arab professor caught my attention. He summarized the events in the Middle East by saying: "The U.S. needs an enemy. With the end of the Cold War with the USSR, they found another one: Islam." My intense reaction at the time explains why this stuck in my mind: First, I was shocked to hear an educated man talk in such simplistic terms based on a false assumption (that the U.S. needs an enemy.) Then, I concluded with a tinge of anxiety that the "Arab point of view" he claimed to espouse was only Iraqi propaganda aimed at muddling the conflict behind the invasion of Kuwait, and at reformulating it into the mythical fight between the forces of evil (the Great Satan of the West) and the forces of goodness (Islam). In addition to feeling strong emotions, I was thinking and commenting to myself on various of the "professor's" points. Finally, I made it my goal to remember the remark, and my reaction to it, as an example to give to my students.

By retelling my memory I reinforce it, dwelling on this or that aspect. It is interesting that my husband never even noticed the remark. And as for my students, the day after I told them the story they repeated quite different versions of it corresponding to their preconceptions. No one could recapture the main idea nor my comments. They remembered my emotions and that I quoted an Arab scholar. Some expressed their ideas on the Middle East. I was only moderately astonished, since I hardly expect an audience to remember everything I say. Attention is frail! It fluctuates and clings to some personal meanings. More-over, people were probably saturated by then with media comments on the Gulf War. All this illustrates in one example the distortion of memories by their underlying subjectivity.

18. Why do people report the same episode differently?

Memory expert Elizabeth Loftus explains it like this: "It's be-cause often we do not see things as they are." Could it be that a magic filter, shaped by personality components, is silently at work? The selectivity of memory seems mysterious to anybody who does not know him/herself. Indeed, because memory is subjective, and most of the time it operates without objectivity constraints, our recollections reveal who we are—our priorities, our opinions, our culture, our prejudices. This is particularly true when there is no time to think, as is the case in situations lasting only a few seconds. Efforts at objectivity require time and observation training. Only in certain contexts such as work or studies, where objective criteria are clearly set, do we see anything like a uniform standard of what information is to be retained. But even in these cases, one notices differences in interpretation or emphasis. The reason is that memory operates on two levels—emotional and rational—both interdependent. The control we have over them is partial and relative. I am reminded of an American play entitled *Bar None:* A murder is committed on stage and the actors refuse to cooperate with the detective, who then turns to the audience and asks a few by-standers to tell what they saw. Everyone seems to have seen something else, particularly when it comes to details. This is typical of ordinary attention, which is passive and unfocused. This mechanism can be complemented by multiple, active ob-servations. You can train yourself to focus on, observe, and remember a scene using objective criteria, as do drama critics and detectives.

Even history does not escape the subjectivity of those who report it. A good example is the Japanese film director Kura-sawa's story of Rashomon, in which several persons retell differ-ent versions of the same sequence of events, so that one leaves the movie theater uncertain about what really happened. Some-times, as every criminal attorney knows, it is impossible to know the truth behind the multifaceted facts.

19. Should one distrust one's memory?

It is not always wise to swear by Jove. Your memory may play tricks on you. In the preceding question I used the image of a "magic filter" to show how, passively and unconsciously, each person makes a different selection of which elements to retain. You really ought to beware of your memory's subjective and subconscious side. Eyewitnesses rarely agree on what happened. They often contradict one another and may even make false accusations. We tend to see what we expect to see, especially when there is no time to think. Prejudices take over and lead to a premature conclusion: For example, in the case of a street crime in the United States, the aggressor "must have been" a young black man—everybody "knows" that, don't the statistics "confirm" it? The particulars of the case are not taken into account when an event is perceived but not "objectively" analyzed. In places where tension runs high, as is so often the case in Jerusalem, it is frequently difficult if not impossible to tell who initiated the violence during a confrontation because both parties to the conflict have registered more subjective elements than objective ones. Even the films of reporters are not infallible, because in many cases they do not retrace the entire sequence of events or are taken from different angles, introducing distortions. By comparing several reports and interviews it is possible to reach a likely truth, but rarely a certain one. It is always shocking to see people condemned to death on the word of a single witness claiming perfect recall.

Unless you have had the leisure and distance to observe the event from start to finish, it is doubtful you can be objective. By becoming less emotional, more relaxed, and more observant, you will gain objectivity. Specific training is helpful, as demonstrated by police officers or private detectives who are able to identify in split-seconds faces, vehicles (including their registration numbers), and other key details.

20. How come I can remember events from twenty years ago, but not what I had for breakfast?

This question obviously concerns people of a certain age; I have heard it mainly from people over the age of 50. (At 20, one remembers little from infancy, but then, this seems only natural: Early childhood memories are notoriously vague and uncertain, most of them relying on parents' stories or old photographs seen several times over the years.)

Paradoxically, it may prove easier to retrieve an older memory than a new one. The explanation is age-related: New recordings in older people are not as reliable (see questions on aging), which hits particularly the memory of the recent past. The events of everyday life leave only a faint trace, whereas the ones from the past, registered under better conditions, left top-quality memory traces. Possessing fewer good-quality recordings of more-recent vintage, the elderly tend to rehash the past ones, all the more so because these come back effortlessly through recognition, an easy type of recall.

Memories of long ago are often brought back to consciousness by involuntary memory, as Marcel Proust wrote in his well-known account of "the madeleine episode": One day as the author was dipping a so-called madeleine biscuit into his tea, he had a delightful surprise. The taste triggered feelings and memories from his childhood at his aunt's, including her garden, which he poetically described at length in *Remembrances of Things Past*, finishing with the famous sentence: "Combray and its surroundings, everything taking shape and volume sprung out, city and gardens, from my cup of tea." We have all experienced such moments, if in a more prosaic way. With a prompter (your senses or thoughts), it is easy to trigger memories, whether recent or past. This is why it is essential to have planted good cues at the time of recording.

If you indulge in a delicious meal that you have been looking forward to, you will remember it. The more you love eating or cooking, the more you will remember specific dishes, especially if you commented on them.

When a situation is exceptional, it mobilizes on the emotional and intellectual levels all the mental processes. Thus, when asking the question above, one might not realize that one is comparing two different entities. Memory traces, whether old or new, are of different quality, depending on how much **elaboration** went into them. Since spontaneous organizational processes diminish with age, conscious effort becomes more critical to recording new information. Moreover, there are different ways to access memories: with cues, or without them. Involuntary-recognition memory is easy at any age because it is prompted by a cue, whether sensory or intellectual; by contrast, the memory elicited voluntarily on the spot isn't. As you see, there is no such thing as equality of memories.

21. Do memory complaints often coincide with retirement?

Yes, especially among those who have not prepared themselves for it. With any reduction of activities comes a commensurate drop in mental stimulation. When you lack the motivation work provides, your need to remember specific information dwindles; the consequences of forgetting are now minor. Goals disappear, and those that replace them are vague. Instead of reading an article to extract work-related specific information, one reads in general, without focus, "for pleasure." Add to this the depression factor that often comes with retirement (in men in particular), and it is easy to understand why people are more vulnerable to memory troubles at this time of transition. Once new activities—the more challenging the better—have replaced work, memory gets reactivated around them.

To motivate your memory it is mandatory that you define goals, if only to talk about this book or that movie or TV show to someone. If you want to record more information, ask yourself questions and express your reactions in an inner monologue, which will turn you from passive to active. Take into account your friends' interests: "Allen would find this exhibit on American painting interesting. I would point out to him how in Edward Hopper's work, there is no communication between the characters nor with the viewer. They stare in an indefinite void without looking at anything in particular. This produces a feeling of alienation, of lack of communication in the city, where so many people come close to one another yet ignore and perhaps avoid one another. A main theme: loneliness amidst the crowd." If you are not going to see your friend right away, strengthen the memory trace by jotting down your comments on paper. The best time for doing it is just after thinking of it. The notes force you to elaborate on the subject more than you would otherwise, and they can be referred to later (the all-important process of **review**).

22. Does living alone affect memory?

Yes, especially in the elderly, because they lack human contacts. When you live alone, memory is handicapped by the lack of the constant need to use it. While the young manage to challenge memory and use it anyway, older persons tend to let it go to pot. As their needs diminish, they attest to not using their memory much "these days." As one 80-year-old lady confessed sadly: "What do I care about time and date, I live in my own bubble and nobody else cares, either." Said another: "I am not sure of remembering my errands, but it does not matter, I'll end up buying something to eat."

Depressive thoughts often go hand in hand with loneliness, which in part explains the problem of impaired memory function among older people. In addition, living alone, by limiting communication, deprives you of the opportunity to exchange information with others and of the stimulation of normal conversation, which commonly triggers recall of many things. In shared living, one has more responsibilities, more goals: "I must bring Joe's jacket to the cleaners." Or "I will tell Michelle about this anti-dandruff shampoo." Memory is linked to activity, itself linked to interaction. With fewer reasons to use it, the memory gets rusty and shrinks.

On the other hand, it should be said, when one lives alone one must assume all the responsibilities: "It is exhausting," a divorcee told me. "Now I have to remember twice as many things!" Or: "Since my husband died, my memory has been crushed under the weight of all the things I need to attend to." In a family setting, responsibilities are shared: "You take care of the house, I take care of the finances, you plan the leisure activities, I mind the kids' homework," etc. If these are your circumstances, try to make the most of it. The extra stimulation, if not too stressful, is good for your memory.

23. Does the saying "use it or lose it" apply to memory?

Yes, it does! To cultivate your memory, you must, first, want to do it and, second, act upon your desire. The older you get, the more important it is to participate consciously in the memory process. By surrounding yourself with all kinds of stimuli—visual (objects), auditory (music), and others—you stimulate many recollections. Sensory stimuli trigger recall; for instance, it is easy to remember past pleasures and friends by looking at photographs or gifts from them. (I enjoy writing with a pen, or eating with a spoon, that a dear friend has given me.) It is in everybody's reach to make the most of the senses by developing them through the use of such reminders. Train yourself to expand your sense of smell by smelling and comparing many scents, from the obvious (perfume and flowers) to all kinds of substances—wood, plastic, leather, whatever things are made of. Do the same with the other senses: touch, taste, hearing. Keep in mind that any activity bringing about reflection will trigger memories through association. As the poet Robert Frost pointed out: "All thought is a feat of association."

People commonly complain about remembering very little of what they have just seen or read, without asking themselves what they have done to remember, or even whether they cared to remember more, or simply whether it was worth remembering. Only if the activity is linked to work or a hobby do we typically make the effort to review, ask questions, or comment—the essence of **depth of processing.** Naturally not everybody is equally efficient; certain students are better learners than others. But in a formal learning situation everyone feels the need to make at least a minimal effort, which is lacking in a leisure context. One must realize that the mental attitude is different. If we are just passing time, we usually read, watch, or listen passively. When watching TV we can be quasi-hypnotized by the screen to the point of sitting there for hours, looking at several shows in a row. In these cases we fail to comment or discuss the contents. On the rare occasion we do it, we remember! A miracle? No. Just make sure you think and comment *immediately* after you watch or read something; you will remember more details. Indulge in an interior monologue, and if possible share your feelings and specific information with someone: "I am going to tell Peter about this article on flying— I know he will be interested." (When you decide to *tell* him about it rather than simply pass it to him, you take the responsibility for summarizing it and analyzing the most interesting ideas. Your friend will appreciate your interest.) Get into the habit of discussing movies after watching them, whether at home or a cafe, as Europeans do. Compare them with other movies, plays, books with the same theme. Don't be too critical about your comments. They help your memory no matter how bright or dim they are. Exchanging ideas stimulates mental processes. When was the last time you analyzed anything, or had an interesting discussion? If you're becoming forgetful, think about comparing what you do nowadays with what you used to do back when you did not complain about your memory. You will see that you can recreate the same behavior if you want to. Mental activity makes the whole difference. Using your memory will prevent you from losing it.

24. Does memory diminish with age?

Yes, but not in a dramatic way. People start complaining about their memory in their thirties. Subjective impression, or reality? A little of both? First, try to determine the objectivity of these "new losses" by placing the problem into perspective: "Was I ever good at remembering the things (names, places, dates, prices, numbers, people, complete the list) that I complain about today? Answer as honestly as possible, and ask the opinions of those close to you. Compare your answers. Chances are your impression is mostly subjective: Have you ever walked into a room and asked yourself suddenly what you went there for? Of course! It happens to everybody at any age. At 30, one does not give it much thought. At 40, one starts worrying: "UH, OH . . . Am I starting to slip?" At 60, watching for the slightest sign of memory loss, one notices many and panics, concluding it must be the prelude to Alzheimer's disease. The curve of depreciation of your memory follows the curve of your anxiety.

While it is true that memory has suffered a decline of about 30 percent by age 70, it may continue to function normally with some help. Since the spontaneous mechanisms are no longer reliable, you must switch to active voluntary processes, participating in the recording, storage, and recall of information. First let us identify the real changes; then, let us find ways of dealing with them. Here is a list of the most common complaints. You will probably find yours. By checking the table of contents you will see that I treat them all, because they concern almost everyone.

- memory in general: "I forget everything!"
- names and faces
- words: "I have it on the tip of my tongue!"
- appointments
- lost objects: "I lose my glasses, my keys . . ."
- readings: "I immediately forget what I read."
- losing the thread of ideas (due to an interruption or a digression while talking)
- what people have said
- places
- directions and instructions
- numbers

This check-up was essential, for it both reduces your anxiety and allows you to target your real problems and find specific solutions. In general, memory adjusts to life changes and remains functional until old age—provided it continues being used. It shrivels with the loss of motivation, but often recycles itself into new areas: You may have forgotten the foreign language you were once fluent in, but you are learning the computer language necessary to your new job. We seldom have an objective perspective, because we dwell on what we forget instead of what we remember. It is not uncommon to see people itemize very accurately a list of all their memory lapses of the week, without any notes! Likewise, people commonly say, "I forgot," when they are referring to something they have actually *remembered*, just in the nick of time.

Research into what goes through older people's minds during their memory efforts indicates that anxious and depressive thoughts too often monopolize the process: "Too many details to register . . . It goes too fast! I cannot hear everything . . . I have already forgotten his name . . . It's too complicated!" some say. In reality, because of all the worrying, they are using only one-third of their capacity. Therefore, if it is true that memory capacity is superior among the young, this is partly because it is fully utilized; less sensitive to interferences, not feeling insecure about their memory, younger people can concentrate on several things at the same time without anxiety creeping in. Our studies have shown that once anxiety and depression are out of the way, the minds of older subjects are free to use their entire capacity, which is more than enough to answer their needs. Only then can they learn general principles to improve attention and strategies to facilitate recall. With these new tools in hand, many function better than ever, because they consciously do what pays off. In everyday life one notices how unobservant people are, no matter what their age. It has been said that in average young people use only 10 percent of their intelligence.

Anybody can do better than that, by developing observation skills that transform attention into concentration, leading to more organization. If you make vague, foggy recordings, you should not be surprised to get vague, foggy recall. *It is at the time of recording that you have the most control over your memory.*

Finally, one observation: Those who show more satisfaction about their memory are more relaxed about it. Not doubting they can trust it, they use it well in their activities; and rather than lament their minor forgetfulness, they congratulate themselves for all they remember. They are active, too busy to be preoccupied by the deficits associated with aging. Feeling young is acting young.

25. How does aging affect memory?

The diagnostic term "age-associated memory impairment" was coined by the National Institute of Mental Health to define the changes that cause memory problems in the course of *normal* aging, as opposed to pathological changes. The older person is likely to experience reduced perception, more vulnerability to interferences, difficulty doing several things at the same time (divided attention), a shorter attention span, and difficulty visualizing and using mental imagery (for example, older people dream less often), all of which mainly affect the recording process. The reduction of metabolism slows down the brain during both recording and recall, which take longer, and also affects spontaneous organization, making new learning increasingly difficult. However, for this declining spontaneous organization one can substitute *learned* strategies to facilitate recall. For each change occurring with age, I shall propose an alternative: For the failing spontaneous processes, we may substitute voluntary awareness. It is as if we were shifting from automatic to manual; after you have learned the mechanisms taught in this book, you will be able to intervene during both the recording and recall stages by exercising **selective attention.** After you make the initial effort at awareness, new habits will develop that facilitate memorization.

Given the fact that there are more individual differences among the old than the young, it may be wise to revise your vocabulary. Instead of saying that it is "normal" to experience memory problems with aging, we should say that it is "common" to do so, and also that it does not mean "disease" (as in Alzheimer's disease). Miscellaneous research in aging has shown that disease, although more frequent with aging, is not caused by it. Many healthy centenarians have proven it. Some people simply are not afflicted by these "age-associated" deficits, and others learn how to compensate, taking them in stride. Everybody can do the same.

26. How do metabolic changes affect memory?

The gradual slowdown of metabolism in turn slows down your responses to stimuli. The resulting split-second lag in reaction time is often resented by people used to thinking fast and acting immediately. Apart from the longer time it takes for recording and recalling, it becomes increasingly difficult to choose the most important stimuli; consequently it is harder to get to work and to organize material. Here is where good work habits make a difference. The discipline to remain seated at your desk in the absence of immediate inspiration helps concentration. No matter how many extraneous thoughts occur, your attention will eventually be redirected toward the subject by the presence of books, documents, and so forth.

The above-mentioned change of metabolism is mirrored by a change in precision: At the physical level, gestures are less precise, attention less focused. This sometimes translates into foggy thinking or sloppy execution of tasks. As attention gets more fragile, it becomes difficult to juggle several things simultaneously: Reading and listening at the same time requires more effort, to the point of becoming problematic. One is more sensitive to interruptions, distractions, and mental digressions.

The age-associated reduction of nerve-cell activity is probably the source of the saying that as people get older they are less creative. There are, of course, numerous exceptions, who continue their activities without worrying about the speed at which they execute them. Whether virtuoso musicians, orchestra conductors, or common folks, as long as they have the energy to maintain the rhythm of the activity everything goes smoothly. No matter what your age, as Agatha Christie's detective genius Hercule Poirot likes to point out, "one cannot hurry the little grey cells." Speaking of speed, it is interesting to note that some new intelligence tests do not give it so much importance. One cannot deny the fact that creative thinking takes time. Albert Einstein was a slow thinker, yet it did not prevent him from demonstrating his intelligence right up to the end of his life.

The NASA space-shuttle accident of the 1980s, in which several U.S. astronauts were killed, was attributed to the speed with which the mission was thrown together to comply with the timetables of the companies renting space aboard the shuttle. In the realm of thought as in that of physical reflexes, the risk of error is proportional to the speed. The most important thing is to find your own rhythm, and accept it. Taking time to think will result in fewer errors.

With the passage of years, we can substitute for speed the systematic use of thinking strategies. By relying on judgment rather than pure recall, we trigger memories without fear of failure. For judgment calls for experience and imagination, both of which bring about spontaneous associations. Anyone can develop and exploit his/her associative memory. This mental faculty remains intact in normal aging. In primitive societies, the elders enjoyed considerable prestige. In our complex modern societies, where constant change in technology is everywhere, the elderly's experience is not so relevant or usable;

therefore it is not valued anymore. This devaluation may be wrong for other than moral reasons: In many fields, knowledge of the principles of commerce or pedagogy is transferable to many fields. On the human psychological level, it is evident that only experience helps put judgment in perspective.

27. Is it possible to restore memory in people over 55?

Absolutely! As we have seen above, it is possible to restore sufficient memory capacity by getting rid of the two major villains, anxiety and depression, through **information and relaxation training.** The results of thirteen years of research on teaching memory techniques to people over 55 prove that it is possible to do so, provided one learns to identify the changes due to normal aging and deal with them individually. To counteract reduced attention, we aim at developing **selective attention** through **observation training.** To reactivate a fading visual memory, we learn to form mental pictures and bring them back to consciousness in a voluntary mode. To the growing lack of spontaneous mental organization, we respond by learning specific recall strategies. And we see results, ranging from the good to the spectacular. Yes, you can teach an old dog new tricks, if you adhere to a proven method. Introducing mnemonics—those magical systems of cues facilitating recall of names and faces, lists, numbers—to older people has to follow a sequence: first, a "pre-training" addressing the above-mentioned changes; then, the mnemonic training.

While reaction speed diminishes with age, judgment and vocabulary remain intact in normal aging. A young person often has to imagine situations in order to make decisions. An older person can evaluate the present in relation to the past, which may take more time but often proves to be more accurate and more valuable. But maximizing your memory in middle and later years is also a matter of developing new, memory-facilitating habits—in particular, attention management. The mental attitude must change: Instead of counting on unconscious memory processes, you deliberately step in. By consciously managing your memory, you participate in its operations and remember what you set out to remember. And you should be satisfied with that, rather than pine for an idealized "total recall" that does not exist.

One thing is sure: *It is never too late to learn how to learn better.* For instance, most people find it is more difficult to go back to school after age 40. To the extent that you encounter difficulty, more effort is involved, and more time is needed to assimilate new learning. However, experience is an advantage, for it brings back many spontaneous references that allow you to place the material in a broader context. People can continue to learn if they are motivated. What is new—and very efficient—is our ability to teach them mental strategies that make learning easier. While you can benefit from these strategies at any age, older people need them more. Indeed, tests results from my memory-training classes have shown that the degree of improvement upon training corresponds to the degree of age-related decline.

28. How can I stop blaming my memory and live with its limitations?

By learning—first about memory, then about yourself. Information reduces anxiety. Understanding memory function, accepting how fragile attention is, differentiating between attention problems and retention problems, learning strategies to facilitate recording, storage, and, recall—and, finally, abandoning perfectionism—are the only ways to stop blaming your memory. You learn, for example, that it is normal to forget a telephone number you just looked up unless you dial it immediately. You may start differentiating between this type of short-term memory (also called "working memory"), which can hold up to seven elements at once provided they are repeated until they are used, and long-term memory. Short-term memory, a more superficial kind of encoding, acts like a scratchpad for immediate use. Therefore it does not include depth of processing or storage. Those who lack self-confidence divide a telephone number into chunks and look at them separately. They are ignorant of the above facts about short-term memory, or else they would not dial a number this way for the simple reason that it is not practical to look back and forth.

Memory problems are in part a matter of personality. Some people are never satisfied with their memory, but neither are they with anything else. These are the perfectionists, who are always saying "I should do better!" They notice only their lapses, and never compare them with the vast amounts of information they do remember, without which normal life would be impossible. Instead of castigating yourself for your forgetfulness, look for its cause, and find a way to prevent it from happening next time. My colleague, Stanford professor of psychiatry and memory expert Jerome Yesavage, tells the story of the typical patient rattling off a long list of his memory lapses of the month *without the help of notes.* He has to point this out to the perplexed person, who finally sees the irony of the situation.

Prove to yourself that when you complain of forgetting "everything," you exaggerate: Write down all the things you have remembered throughout the day, and put it next to a list of what you have forgotten to do. By reconciling your "balance-of-lapses" account, you will get rid of that counterproductive negative feeling. You should now be able to evaluate your memory more objectively, and to help it serve you better. Or, from a logical standpoint, consider the complexity of memory function and how it depends on an equilibrium between forgetting and recall. Memory lapses are few if one considers the thousands of operations handled constantly and more or less effortlessly. If your memory answers your needs, isn't that enough? Be kind to yourself, forgiving small lapses but making sure you avoid the big ones. You will be able to do just that after reading this book.

29. How can one maximize one's memory at any age?

When I was a student, my motto was: "Everything is a question of organization!" Perhaps because I do not consider myself super-organized, I never gave it up, although I changed my terminology to: "A method for everything." Avoiding the endless trial-and-error comedy of ordinary experience, you can zoom in on your goal. No matter what the subject—sport, cooking, mechanics, gardening, reading—the techniques and the tools you choose make the difference between frustration or satisfaction, between failure and success.

As in many other domains, it is not the quantity but the quality of memories that count. By exploiting the phenomenon of **selective attention,** everybody can make the most of their brain cells at any age. To demystify your memory, study it: What are its strengths and its weaknesses? Identify and anticipate the situations in which attention cannot be sustained. Accept the fact that memory is subjective, and that personality, mood, environment, and cultural background all determine what you record and what you recall. Understand that your needs and interests strongly affect your motivation to pay attention and to concentrate on a precise target for retention. Are you happy with your concentration? "It depends on the subject. . . . " That is normal! Do you wish to improve it? In general or in specific areas? Which ones? If you do, you will accept readily the following:

- **observation training** (selecting, focusing, analyzing, and commenting at the time information is to be recorded);

- the **pause** (taking the time to become aware of what you are doing);

- **relaxation** (removing anxiety and tension to become more receptive);

- **selective attention** (defining what you want to remember, why, and for how long);

- **image-association** (recording information in the visual mode, as if your mind were a camera, and forging connections between different images by mentally pairing them—later on, thinking of one image will trigger recall of the other);

- **verbal elaboration** (making comments, both intellectual and emotional, on the subject).

With these principles in hand, you will have the necessary tools to use mental strategies, among them mnemonic systems. You will even make up your own "custom-tailored" methods and find they work even better. You will switch from a passive to an active participant, taking charge of recording and recall instead of waiting for the memory processes to do their work unassisted. It is through action that you maximize your memory. You will act more efficiently if you practice voluntary, specific strategies, which will be illustrated in context in the sections that follow.

As a preview, here is an example from everyday life: How do I remember where I parked my car? First, I pause: I become aware of what I am doing, not thinking about what I am going to do next—interrupting the conversation for a few seconds if need be. I close the windows and lock all the doors *consciously,* not automatically. Then I look for visual cues, which I describe to myself: in front of this store, advertisement, tree, etc. An important tip: While leaving the place, I turn around to take a mental picture (image-association) of my car near the *permanent cues* (not the car next to it!) that I will see upon my return. If one does not recognize places, it is often because one has not registered them from the angle at which one will be coming back. Landscapes appear different depending on the point of view. If possible, I involve other senses: smell—restaurant, gas, bushes, trees or flowers; hearing—traffic, cars starting at the lights, music; touch—the temperature of the air. I also make comments: "Parked between the street corner and a driveway—I hope no one hits me!" If I enter a department store, I make sure I take a mental note of the department: "Men's clothing." This will make it easier to go back directly to the car.

A few seconds of skillful observation will save you time. You will be proud of your efficacy and your memory. One success will trigger many others in a domino effect.

2

FOCUSING ATTENTION

You can't recall information you've never recorded in the first place. This section deals with questions about how to sustain and direct your attention so that you record information at a deep level, ensuring a good memory trace.

1. How are memory, motivation, and attention related?

You know that you retain easily what interests you whereas you struggle with what does not. This is proof enough that there is a relation between memory, motivation, and attention. The essential elements of memorization can be illustrated by imagining a chain made of the following links:

Interest/Need ➜ Motivation ➜ Attention ➜ Concentration ➜ Organization

Without interest, there is no motivation to pay attention and concentrate on something specific, thereby organizing one's thinking. No wonder then, that we forget a lot of information that left us indifferent in the first place. Interest is essential in creating the motivation indispensable to sustaining attention.

Interest is related to the personality and the circumstances, and can change with them. Thus we may remember well the price of items we have purchased when under budget restrictions, but not those we bought when we felt we were well off. Likewise, our interest in clothes can fade if our closets are full or the opportunity to wear them has vanished. We will then forget both what we have at home and what we see in the stores. (Incidentally, it is normal to forget what you have stored from one season to the next. That is why I have gotten into the habit of browsing in my closet before I go browsing in the stores: I rediscover barely used treasures loaded with memories. This also creates an opportunity to sort out good and bad memories attached to clothes. Many a time have I gotten rid of an item associated with unpleasant situations. Why activate unpleasant memories by keeping reminders of them?)

There is a difference between working conditions and daily-life conditions.[1] Work dictates necessities and focuses the "lens" of concentration: An editor has to be attentive to style, content, typos; a police officer, to suspicious-looking individuals or traffic rules being broken. On vacations and in other areas of everyday life this type of attention slackens because the motivation and the goal are not there any more to sustain it. Awareness of what

---

[1] which call on, respectively, "explicit" and "implicit" memory.

we do and why we do it is essential to memory control.

Routine dulls perception so that we do not notice familiar things anymore. Thus, we erroneously invoke the word "forget" when we cannot say the name of the street where a familiar movie theater is. Unless we have recorded cues that described the location, the information was registered only vaguely. If you program vague references, you will remember vague references. (As the software wizards say: garbage in, garbage out.) The truth is, in many cases we are satisfied with approximations such as: "It is close by, not far from here." If you think about it, you will discover many similar examples regarding familiar itineraries and other miscellaneous information, which simply proves the need to consciously select, focus on, and analyze the particulars you want to record. *Attention is conscious, not reflex;* it is indispensable to the controlled recording of information.

We must learn to differentiate *at*tention problems from *re*tention problems: In one case, recording is deficient to the point of leaving no memory trace; in the other, it is recall that proves weak: The memory trace is there, but there is no cue to retrieve it. Fortunately there is a solution to both problems. Attention can be improved by various means: relaxation, sensory awareness, observation training, intellectual stimulation. Organizational strategies (such as grouping by **categories**) and mnemonics help focus attention. The effect is equivalent to that of being equipped with a magnet to find a needle in a haystack.

2. Is it possible to conquer absent-mindedness and stop misplacing things?

We misplace things for the simple reason we have not paid attention to where we put them. This is not unusual if you tend to be distracted or rather disorganized. Order helps memory; when attention fails, you can assume that you have, by habit, done the right thing: put things in their place. People who are distracted act somewhat like robots! The French author La Bruyere entertained thousands of readers with his description of the absent-minded Menalque:

> Menalque goes downstairs, opens the door to get out, closes it immediately: He notices that he is still wearing his night cap, . . . that his stockings are down around his ankles, that his shirt is hanging over his trousers. . . . It is still he who walks into a church, and mistaking the blind beggar at the door for a column and his cup for a holy-water basin, puts his hand in it, then brings it to his forehead; when suddenly he hears the pillar talk, he starts praying to it. . . .

While the situation described in the second sentence of this quotation is gross and grotesque, the first comes close to the daily reality of absent-minded people. At least Menalque eventually notices the state of his attire, whereas certain people do go out wearing a different-colored sock on each foot, or with their shirt improperly buttoned, or their tie poorly knotted; still others find themselves out in the cold in winter without coat or gloves. It is said that the absent-minded person is "in the clouds"; that is, "elsewhere," in another reality where his mind has taken him. People can and must come out of their bubbles if they want to correct their distraction. If you are a dreamer, if you do not care about what is happening around you, if you are always thinking ahead of what you are doing, you are susceptible to interferences and your attention is restricted. Under these conditions, it is inevitable that you will forget lots of things, because they never get recorded. Far from being a memory deficit, your problem is an attention deficit that dates back to the time of recording. **Automatic gestures** account for most bothersome incidents of forgetfulness in everyday life: You lock the car door without thinking, and cannot recall whether you locked it or not. You add salt to your soup while talking, and shortly afterward you grab the saltshaker again, having "forgotten" your previous gesture. You put your glasses on the table (or on your nose!), and look for them everywhere in your bedroom, where you went for another reason already forgotten!

You must fight distraction with a firm commitment to paying attention—which is relatively easy if you suffer from the consequences of embarrassing episodes of forgetfulness. You can control the situation if you are willing to do so; but if you find it an "OK" personality characteristic and feel no need for change, you will refuse to make the effort to learn strategies that help you control attention.

Several attention-management strategies have given excellent results with subjects of all ages. To break the habit of automatic gestures, you must become aware of what you are doing. The first principle to keep in mind is the **pause.** Set your mind in the "conscious" mode. This allows you to look around and catch visual cues. Before going anywhere, pause and ask yourself these basic questions: "Where am I going? What do I need?" Breathe deeply to dissipate your haste, and answer these questions. You will notice how mastering this principle eliminates much forgetfulness. *Remembering is taking the time to think.*

The second principle of correcting attention deficits derives from an awareness of what you are doing: It is the ability to sustain **concentration** on the present moment. (In research this is referred to as "task-oriented thinking.") Once immersed in your activity, it will be easier to avoid distractions.

The third principle is **anticipation**. In work-related contexts, you can eliminate interferences by getting organized: Ban from your work area all background music, personal photographs, books on subjects other than the one you are working on. The older you get, the more sensitive you are to distractions that interfere with attention. (Many adolescents are still able to study in less-than-ideal conditions such as listening to loud rock music. Notice, however, that these are not typically the best students, who instinctively know better!)

Incidentally, here is another tip to avoid losing your thread of thought: Avoid digressions, another kind of interference. . . . Now where was I? Ah, yes, I was saying that you can control interruptions by anticipating them. The major interruption of modern professional life is the telephone. You will surely agree with me that no one should succumb to the tyranny of the telephone's ring. Why not use an answering machine? If you're not ready for so much technology, it is easy to ask your main callers to let the phone ring six times before hanging up. This will give you time to organize and finish your sentence or turn the gas off in the kitchen, or at least to plant some cue for yourself (a book mark, a note, an object) so that you can pick up where you left off.

By anticipating your distractions, you can prevent them. For instance, to remember if you have taken all your vitamins or medications, get them out of their container, count them, and put them on your breakfast plate; as you swallow each one, become aware of how it feels (some are bigger, some smaller, and each has a different coating and consistency). If you do not consciously organize, you may risk forgetting which one you have already taken and taking it twice. This is most likely to happen when you are sleepy, or in a hurry, or just talking about something else. Beware of situations in which attention is especially fragile, and organize to cover potential slips. Habitual (and therefore conscious-bypassing) **automatic gestures,** haste, worries, stress, fatigue, anxiety, depression and interruptions— the root causes of most memory lapses—are identifiable and predictable most of the time.

The fourth principle: **immediate action.** Do it now, while you're thinking of it. Do you intend to take your umbrella? return a book to the library? bring a picture to a friend you are visiting? Put them with your purse or by the door *at the time you think of it.* Do not procrastinate, and you will avoid many incidents of forgetfulness. Attention starts with prevention.

Another application: Review information *immediately* after having been exposed to it: After meeting people, review their names and miscellaneous relevant details about them; after a lecture, a conference, or a show, make comments about what you found interesting.

Sometimes you will have to hang on to your idea until it is written down or executed, or risk losing it. Do not hesitate to use simple repetition when you are fighting interferences, as is the case when going to a room to look for something. Focusing your thoughts on your goal and commenting to yourself on it suffices to keep it in mind until you reach it: "My address book should be in the drawer of my desk; I hope it is still there!" Visualizing the target adds to your concentration. Use interior monologue to remember an item until you get to it. And do not be too harsh on yourself if, instead, you succumb to your cat's demands to be petted, thereby derailing your attention. One can resist anything but temptation! Absorbed by your cat, you may now wonder what you came to fetch. Rest assured, your idea will return as you mentally retrace what you were doing before the interruption, or physically go back to where you came from—perhaps to your reading. There you will see a visual reminder that will prompt you: Ah, yes, you needed your address book or your glasses. Visual reminders rarely miss their target. Next time you may manage to hang on to your idea until it is executed, and not allow yourself to be distracted. In case you are, accept the distraction and the pleasure it gave you. Distractions, because unpredictable, add charm to life!

3. How can I improve my ability to remember directions and develop a memory for places?

Do you get lost easily? Do you often have the impression that you do not recognize places where you have been? If you answered "yes," chances are you do not pay much attention to your surroundings. Absorbed in your thoughts or your conversation, you do not look around. Therefore you may be unable to retrace your steps to your car. Or worse yet, you fail to recognize the street on which you parked it. It is easy, however, to pause for a "photo stop," recording cues to help you recall the place. This requires only systematic and voluntary action. Think about associating your car with permanent visual cues, and turn around to take a mental shot of the scene as you will see it upon your return. This proves particularly useful while hiking on a trail: To remember it better, record visual cues from *both* directions, as you would see them coming *and* going—they are very different perspectives. Also, make sure that your cues are *permanent* and will be there when you come back: Just as Hansel and Gretel found that their breadcrumb cues had been eaten by the birds, I once managed to lose the marks I had drawn on the snow at cross-country trail intersections, simply because more snow had fallen shortly afterward.

Of course, not everybody has the same difficulty remembering places. There are the "lost souls," and then there are those who have a good sense of direction and like to guide others. The latter are interested in maps, and consult them often. They always record mental cues. If they know the area, they memorize numerous cues; they can give directions accurately, because they spontaneously visualize, and can share their knowledge with others.

By contrast, those who do not have a natural sense of direction have more or less given up on trying to remember places and how to get to them, because it demands too much effort. The surrender is abetted by the eager delegation of this responsibility to those who seem to enjoy it and who remember such information seemingly effortlessly. The problem arises when you are alone! The good news is that it is possible to manage, notwithstanding your natural predisposition. Just imitate the actions, mentioned above, of those who remember. What one does not do spontaneously, one can do voluntarily: Write down directions and review them several times before leaving. This will allow you to recognize the cues. If you know the area, visualize the sites. Memorizing a map requires studying it in detail—which few people know how to do, according to a test given to subjects of all ages in a well-known research project. On this test, only a single subject—an army general and "tactical-operations specialist"—was able to draw the map from memory, because he had mastered the following study strategy and used it all his life: To learn a map, divide it in sections and analyze each section in order, one after the other, starting from the upper left corner and moving horizontally towards the right. Transitions between sections should be studied closely, to allow the visualization of an ever-larger segment of the map. That this exercise proved difficult for most people, except for the general, proves that *strategy* and *practice* are the only tools for memorizing complex images.

To remember sites you visit, you must observe the place with interest, carefully identifying what is peculiar to it, and dwell on strong images, flashing them back from time to time for the sheer enjoyment of mentally traveling back there. I suggest that you follow natural memory, which proceeds from the emotional to the analytic. For instance, to remember a picnic, note first the mood: "We had to hike a long time before finding a shady spot. But the place was lovely, under a big oak tree, with a view of the valley." In so doing, you have already described the visual elements of the site. Continue describing and commenting on the food, the company, the conversation, and add other sensory impressions: touch (temperature, comfort,) smell (grass or lavender), taste (the delicious spinach quiche), and so on. The more you involve the senses, the stronger the memory trace will be. Not only will you be able to retrieve a better memory when you call for it, but by increasing your sensory awareness, you will elicit many more episodes of spontaneous memory. Think of this both at the time of recording and recall.

4. How come I can't remember what I ate for dinner?

Probably because food is not one of your priorities. Or could it be that your spouse fixes your meals, and you are not interested in cooking? You are certainly not one of those who live through their stomachs! Such people do remember the dishes they eat, commenting on them during and after the meal, the conversation revolving around their taste buds. Your mealtime attention is probably turned elsewhere—as is surely the case if you remember the guests, what they said, the place, the service, but not the menu. But if you love good food, you remember the excellent meals, and the flops, too. Interesting test: Do you remember your wedding menu—or, closer in time, your wedding anniversary menu? If you do, you either show an interest in food or were actively involved in its choice or preparation; if not, you may be romantic, or just floating above reality. (If you cannot remember anything precise at all, no comment.)

I have noted that this question seems to preoccupy French people more than Americans. Did you know that among affluent nations, the French spend the greatest portion of their salary on food? For them eating is an art of living. Rather than a function, it has become a lifestyle: To forget what one eats means not appreciating what one eats, one of life's pleasures. It is also offensive to the cook or the hostess. Therefore a food-forgetting Frenchman feels guilty on two counts, experiencing the additional onus of having betrayed his cultural heritage.

But apart from this unusual case, most people remember exceptional meals precisely because they were not ordinary: A delicious rack of lamb, a tasty coucous (or a greasy one) that had to be eaten the Arab way with the fingers, or a Thai dish that burned one's guts, leaves memory traces impossible to erase. (This is confirmed in a story told by my grandfather, who could never forget the joke played on him by colleagues as he arrived in Mexico: They offered him "olives" that were in fact a type of hot chili. He had tears in his eyes whenever he described how these "balls of fire" set his mouth and belly on fire for days!)

The principle behind these stories: *What is different from the norm or appeals to emotions sticks in the memory.* By contrast, what is neutral does not provoke a reaction, and therefore escapes attention and depth of processing. It is up to you to find multiple applications, concentrating on differences and on what touches you to the quick.

5. How come I remember so little from movies, TV shows, exhibits?

This question reflects more your frustration than the degree of your forgetfulness. Was your memory for this particular subject better in the past? How did you use to test it? What did you use to do differently? It is probable that the situations in your life have changed more than your brain has. Are you more tired? in a hurry to the point of not taking the time for a cup of coffee after a movie or a show, thus depriving yourself of the chance to discuss it at the most opportune time—immediately after the event? Do you tend to watch several TV shows in a row, or double features at the movies? Do you take the time to think about them and discuss them with someone?

If you detect a few differences in your behavior, they may explain the changes in your memory performance. Do your friends like exchanging ideas? Many people yearn for their student years (by the way, too often idealized). Without social structure encouraging communication, it is natural to watch shows without trying to remember them, because the only goal is to be entertained at the moment; it may happen that you just mention what the show was about, and no more. Take heart: It is normal to forget 80 percent of what one watches passively, especially if it is not reviewed in the next 24 hours. Without special motivation, one sees without looking. To remember better, you must be actively involved, and make it a point to observe, fix a goal, and ask questions *before, during and after* the event.

(This is called, in clinical jargon, **verbal elaboration,** necessary to **depth of processing** for long-term recall.) Perhaps the simplest goal you can define is that of telling someone about what you've seen as soon as possible. In my opinion, nothing beats discussing a movie right after seeing it, on the way home or in a more leisurely style at a cafe—which I acknowledge is more a feature of the European than the American way of life. What is important is to do it *immediately,* while the memory traces are fresh.

While the questions you can ask yourself in order to "burn" traces into your memory are matters of personal choice, they can be organized by subjects. I suggest following nature, and eliciting subjective responses: "Do I like it or not?" (Or: "Do I find it interesting or not?") Then ask yourself, "*What* is it I like, or find interesting?" This second question leads to analysis and comment. In general we best remember what is striking and what we have made a personal comment about.

It is impossible to remember "everything," because memory is subjective and selective. The illusion of having recorded more than one really has is the source of many an unjust complaint. If you can identify and define clearly what you want to retain, you will manage to do so most of the time. Of course it is possible to develop observation skills and remember more than you do at the present. Memory "miracles" do not really exist; they can be explained by strategies you can analyze and learn to apply. It boils down to developing good mental habits that facilitate memorization: Rather than expect recall to simply "happen" through involuntary associations, *make* it happen by calling on categories: subject, mood, colors, emotions. At the time of recording, be more aware, more receptive, more curious, more analytic, raising numerous questions and trying to answer them as you keep on reading or looking. In so doing, you record a top-quality memory trace. For gaining (or *regaining*) control of your memory, the more strategies using the senses, emotions, and intellect, the better.

Before blaming your memory, admit that, consciously speaking, you haven't done much to remember what you complain about forgetting. Did you know that the average time people spend in front of a picture at a museum is only six seconds? No wonder they retain so little: This is just long enough to identify what they are looking at. Once you identify what you are interested in, it will be easy to focus on it and remember it—but you will have spend some time on it. Observation training (the only guarantee of depth of processing), requires practicing awareness, selective attention, analysis, comparison of differences and resemblances, and the formulation of personal comments. (See Question #20, this section.)

6. How come I can't remember whether I locked the door, whether I shut off the gas, or where I parked my car?

Probably because you have exercised an **automatic gesture**—a habitual routine bypassing consciousness—and therefore it was never registered. Or you may have been interrupted, or you were trying to do too many things at the same time. If your mind is on something else (often on what you are going to do next), it is not on what you are doing. To avoid memory slips, you must learn to control your attention in situations where it is most fragile, as is the case when you are in a hurry, stressed, or preoccupied. You still can manage to do so by integrating the **pause** into your daily habits: Before going anywhere, pause, breathe deeply, and ask yourself this basic question: "What am I doing?" Dwell on it, answering immediately by just looking around you and becoming aware of your erstwhile-automatic gestures, commenting on your actions: "I am locking the doors, turning the lights off, checking the gas." This way, you will record information in a conscious mode, paving the way for voluntary memory instead of counting on the more unreliable involuntary memory. Paradoxically, the more reflex good attention habits become, the better you can prevent automatic gestures. (Please ponder the nuance!)

7. To what extent can one control attention?

Notwithstanding individual differences, *what characterizes attention in general is its fragility.* For instance, did you know that the attention span of an audience on a subject of interest is twenty minutes, *maximum?* That is why in public speaking it is important to convey the essential part of the message first. A good class or brilliant speech takes into account these precious moments of receptivity, after which attention slackens naturally so that one needs to resort to stratagems—pauses, variation in the speed of delivery and tone of voice, striking examples, anecdotes, humor, a change of subject, or activity—to bring it back. Observe how society has taken "preventive" measures to avoid mishaps: Official papers usually need to be signed in two places. Checks must mention the sum in numbers and in letters. A great number of business envelopes have printed reminders such as, "Have you signed your check? written your account number on it?" These force the reader to check what he is doing. Ubiquitous signs in planes and trains remind people not to leave personal belongings behind. Pilots must follow procedures from checklists during the crucial operations of takeoff and landing.

Most accidents are the result of human error, not mechanical failure. Most of these errors stem from attention deficits—such as that of the driver who killed three cyclists not long ago while changing an audio cassette as she drove on a narrow windy road near Palo Alto, California. A fraction of inattention was enough to cause the tragedy, which could have been avoided had she anticipated the presence of bikes or pedestrians on the road and postponed fiddling with the cassette until she came to a straight patch with good visibility. The accidents of memory are analogous to those on the road: While you cannot escape them all, you can avoid most of them by developing safety reflexes based on anticipation, observation, and conscious selective attention.

By organizing ahead of time, you can reduce the number of incidents of forgetfulness; but when unpredictable events happen, analyzing the circumstances may help you to forgive yourself. For instance, once I "forgot" a cardigan on one of France's celebrated high-speed trains. Suffering from a back injury, I had asked a gentleman to take my suitcase down from the storage rack, but he kept on chatting with me until the train came to a halt. When he hastily grabbed the suitcase, the wheel cart that was attached to it fell apart, and I had to rush to put it back on before darting towards the exit door. The unexpected had happened, leaving me at the mercy of my automatic gestures. Already wearing my purse on a sling and my coat on my back, I had neither the time nor the presence of mind to look around and check whether I had left something on the rack. Once on the platform, I noticed immediately that I was missing my cardigan—but it was too late. Those fast trains stop only for one minute!

The moral of the story? Don't blame your memory for your lack of attention, especially in situations where it cannot be sustained. Rather, congratulate yourself on having been able to concentrate on what was important—in my case, my back, and putting the wheels back on the suitcase to avoid straining it. If you are organized, you may be able to anticipate many such episodes, and thereby to face them more calmly. Since the train incident, I have learned to prepare, put away everything I am not wearing, and make sure that my luggage is in front of the door well in advance of the time of arrival. I have also become more assertive and now dare to interrupt the conversation to make it clear how important it is to me to be ready a little early.

However, there are a certain number of situations, fortunately less frequent, in which attention cannot be sustained. The worst is depression. In this state, the mind is monopolized by negative thoughts. The same occurs with anxiety and extreme situations—when under emotional stress, when interrupted, when digressions occur, when in a hurry or rushing. In all these scenarios, your mind is not on what you are doing, because it is absorbed by some other task that has priority in your psyche. It is difficult to reverse your emotional priorities.

In general, we fight anxiety by orienting our thinking to the task we need to concentrate on. Rather than dwell on your emotions ("Oh, God! I am going to miss the station."), which prevents focusing, think fast on the immediate action to take (put the wheel cart back on the suitcase).

A last point: Attention is destroyed by different chemical substances such as alcoholic beverages, barbiturates and other sleeping pills, and stimulants.

8. Does fatigue diminish attention, hence memory?

Yes indeed, just as stress, alcohol, sleeping pills, and other drugs causing drowziness do. Also keep in mind that jet-lag diminishes judgment ability, an impairment of which few business people seem aware. When you are tired, it is better to postpone difficult tasks and decisions requiring all your attention. If this is not possible, try using the attention strategies I've proposed earlier in this section—even the ones you find coarse: reminders such as an alarm clock or watch, a sticker note in a strategic place. Of course you can enlist someone's help whenever you feel under the weather: "Dear, make sure I don't forget to call Josephine before going to bed." This latter suggestion, however, is the least reliable of all, since the other person's memory may be worse than your own! In general, try acting on something right when you think of it. In the preceding example it might make sense to make that call right here and now, rather than postpone it for two hours and count on someone to remind you of it. Better to rely on yourself than on others. At least place a note on your pillow.

When you feel drained, take a short ten- to fifteen-minute nap or do some relaxation exercises. You will feel renewed. Just remember to do it!

9. Do circadian rhythms influence attention?

Yes, sleep studies in the U.S. and abroad show that sleeping seven or eight hours in a row is not enough to guarantee quality of rest. Other conditions must be favorable: no noise, no lights, and regularity of sleep time conforming to the body's natural circadian rhythms—generally, nighttime. People who work night shifts are less efficient, even if they sleep an adequate number of hours during the day. Night is inauspicious for working: More accidents or errors of judgment in the workplace occur at night. Did you know that you are less likely to survive an operation performed during the night? Studies of airplane pilots reveal deficits in performance due to jet-lag, which is simply a disruption of circadian rhythm. Airline employees, in spite of international scheduling rules, are always crossing time zones. Most people, however, can plan to travel by day and sleep regular hours to guarantee restful sleep. (Here, too, quality and regularity matter more than quantity.)

10. Does attention alone guarantee recall?

No, paying attention is not enough to guarantee recall, especially long-term recall, on demand. Attention is the *sine qua non* condition for recording information, but it is necessary to store that information along with cues that will prompt recall later on. Among the three operations memory performs—**recording, storage,** and **recall**—the latter is the most difficult. The art of memory resides in organizing the storage of traces so that they will be easy to access with the help of cues. One learns to do that by classifying first what one perceives *in a sensory mode:* For example, to remember a restaurant I like, I record the decor, the furniture, the colors, the light, the smells (cooking, flowers, wood, etc.), the comfort of the chairs, the texture of the tables (wood grain, metal, marble, plastic) or tablecloths, and music or noise (certain places have poor acoustics, which makes them noisy and unsuitable for conversation); and of course, I take good mental notes on the best dishes. In this example I manage to integrate the five senses (which is not always possible, depending on the context); in so doing, the thought processes follow **categories.** There are all kinds of categories, and it is natural to proceed from sensory and affective categories to more intellectual ones, including judgment and appreciation.

To facilitate recall, file information in categories that will always be easy to access at any time. Imagine that the mind is a camera taking mental pictures of miscellaneous images, clustering and classifying them on different levels. (In fact that is exactly what takes place when we remember.) First, define a goal: What is it I really want to remember? Why? For how long? Then, consciously work on the recording: *Observe, select, focus, and analyze, and then comment.* Train yourself by using these techniques with places you patronize or visit, with the news, magazine articles, even people or conversations. For instance: "I am going to tell Christine about the good weather news. There is snow in the mountains, and we can go skiing this weekend." With the responsibility of communicating a message, one listens better, watches better, and tries to remember more details. Consciously use all the strategies you know to take more mental pictures of what you see on your TV screen—for example, satellite shots of clouds traveling across the country during the weather report, to help you focus on temperature patterns; you may even catch certain terms as I did recently when the weatherman humorously qualified two storms making their way towards California as "macho and wimp." You will get used to commenting on what you find interesting: "Wonderful, it's snowing now! Let's hope the temperature doesn't change. With a little bit of luck the snow will have stopped by the time we get there, and we can ski on "powder." All these mental operations process information in depth for long-term recall. Visualization and verbal elaboration are the two key components known to leave a high-quality memory trace. By using both emotional and intellectual resources, you can control the recording, storage, and recall of valuable information.

11. Even with focused attention, do we leave things out?

Of course: One has only to see what is retained from listening to a dialogue, a speech, a conference, a book, or a TV show. Attention, like memory, is selective, and therefore subjective. Information is filtered by our knowledge of the world, our culture, our prejudices, our personal references. One person will notice this or that item, another will not. Test yourself by recording the news on a tape recorder, and compare what you remember with a friend you've recruited to listen. First, you will notice, you remember more information when you make the conscious effort to do so. Second, you and your friend are likely to remember the information differently. During the Gulf War I mentioned to my husband that I was struck by the comment of an Iraqi soldier who declared to a Western journalist: "Of course I tortured people, what do you think, I am a soldier!" His amazement at the question, and his air of innocence, made such an impression on me that I indulged in many comments about the immorality of a leader who trains his army to become unscrupulous like him, so that soldier and torturer are one and the same thing in the mind of his troops. This loss of conscience made me go on and on, focusing on this particular detail at the expense of the rest of the news item. Note here the selective-attention process based on my emotion, the expression on the soldier's face, the cultural references, the personal comments, the communication, and the quotation. Chances are I will remember it for a long time, especially if I continue citing this example.

Human memory is subjective; that is why, in a way, so is history. Omissions are inevitable, because the selective attention of historians is not always conscious. (One speaks, for instance, of a "Marxist point of view.") Rather than describing events, they interpret them. It is only through exposing oneself to different points of view that one gets at the facts.

12. Are memory traces stored permanently, or do they get erased with time?

From the time of Plato up to the 19th century, it was assumed that all memories were permanently stored in the mind, ready to be reawakened at any time. During the last century, the observations of neurologists on the way memories were stored gave rise to the theory of functional localization, which associates precise functions (vision, speech, emotions) with specific areas of the brain. When one of these regions is affected, one notices problems in a particular function.

The complexity of the mind, however, makes it possible for some people with localized brain injuries to transfer certain functions to other areas. This recognition has led to a new emphasis on nerve-cell connections rather than the place they emanate from.

Moreover, in normal memory function some perceptions are stressed at the expense of others through selective attention—only a few will be reviewed and prevented from sliding downhill into the unconscious mass of useless information. Thus, memories are fragmentary.

The accuracy of recall is difficult to prove in any case, since so many subjective elements are imbedded in memories. Neurologist Oliver Sacks reports on "memory-artist" Franco Magnani, whose whole life revolves around his attempts, through painting, to reconstruct his childhood village of Pontito, in the Tuscan hills of Italy. Even though Magnani's eidetic memory is remarkable in its recall of details of still-existing buildings and streets, comparisons with recent photographs show distortions due to the way Magnani the child perceived what he saw. His emotions colored the stones, rooftops, and window frames, and bathed the village in a golden glow of the childhood that Magnani stuggled to rekindle. The artistic distortion parallels the distortions of memory.

Long before the research studies of the 1930s began to stress the importance of the brain's limbic system (the physiological "Ground Zero" of the emotions), Freud had noticed how essential emotion was in the evocation of memories. Nowadays, we believe that memories are eroded by time, partly because of disuse but also partly because they are slightly altered with each recall. In his book, *The Invention of Memory*, Israel Rosenfield explains that we are not dealing with rigid images but with reconstructions of these images, each one a pure product of the imagination, a vision of the past adapted to the present. The biological foundation of such an understanding of memory has been described by Nobel laureate neurobiologist Gerald Edelman in his Darwinian theory of how the nervous system classifies sensory information: The most meaningful information survives. Memory is Darwinian in its pragmatism. Each individual creates his/her own world by reacting to it differently, and eliminating personally meaningless elements.

One does not remember equally well everything one has registered. Certain memories have left stronger or weaker traces, depending on how they came to be used. For instance, cramming may hold information until the exam, after which the magic slate is erased. What remains in long-term memory has been recorded differently, in depth, with multiple references that allowed the information to be integrated systematically. But, as we have seen, memory traces do not remain intact; every time one is recalled, it appears in a different context, eliciting a comment on one or another aspect. When stored again, this memory has been altered by the new recall, during which some elements have been expanded at the expense of others not even summoned. The more time that elapses, the more chances of manipulation of the memory trace.

Moreover, we can never know what remembering "everything" means, for in everyday life there exists no objective physical proof to define what has been registered in the first place. (Even photography rarely translates exactly what we have seen.) Scientific studies on reading do, however, impose certain objective criteria: They reveal a considerable loss after only 48 hours. A mere 20 percent of what has been read remains, and that is only the main idea. Details and developments vanish rapidly unless they are picked up and reinforced by personal reflections or comments that integrate this information into contexts meaningful to the individual. The more one "grafts" associations onto a subject, the more files of categories can be opened later on to grant access to the memory trace. The better the storage, the easier the recall. Another important factor is the frequency of review of information: The more often I quote an example, the more easily it comes to mind when I need it.

Finally, let statistics talk: According to a survey from the National Institute for Development and Administration at the University of Texas, people will remember only:

- 10 percent of what they read;
- 20 percent of what they hear;
- 30 percent of what they see;
- 50 percent of what they see *and* hear;
- 70 percent of what they say;
- 90 percent of what they do *and* say.

You may well be startled by these statistics, which reflect spontaneous performance in everyday situations. But you can beat the average. Just apply the principles of good retention repeated throughout this book. For instance, recording information in more than one sensory mode leaves a better trace—

remembering 50 percent of what one "sees and hears" suggests that the combination is superior to just hearing (20 percent) or just seeing (30 percent). In addition, motivation, goal setting, and the passage to action guarantee better recall. You will remember 90 percent of what you "do and say," but very little of what you read passively (10 percent)—unless you put in the effort implied by the term "studying."

13. Why do we sometimes remember insignificant details but forget the essential?

This is a difficult question, because it is not always clear what is "essential," this judgment being more subjective than objective. We perceive the world first through perception and only then through the intellect, so it is no wonder that certain details stand out. This selectivity reflects our personality, which in turn is an expression of our culture. So, rather than making a general statement, it would be appropriate to find out the special meaning of a particular detail to an individual. Certain people remember technical details, others esthetic ones, in accord with their education and their turn of mind. It is interesting to ponder the kinds of things we remember and to observe our own tendencies or professional biases. For instance, a film critic does not watch a movie like the average spectator. In an interview with Pauline Kael of *The New Yorker* magazine, Woody Allen deplores the habit critics have of taking notes during films. In Allen's opinion, this intellectual distance is an aberration, for it prevents the viewer from apprehending the subject in a global manner, at once visual, emotional, and intellectual. Thus, he argues, critics may give too much importance to certain elements and neglect others. While we can understand the filmmaker's frustration, we must admit that the critic's distortions may be no worse than the spectator's. Criteria may differ, the critic's being more defined and limited, but when going to the movies, everyone is struck by spectacular scenes on which the camera lingers—for instance, Charlie Chaplin eating his shoe in *The Gold Rush,* or the murder scene in the shower in *Psycho.* (Hitchcock, the master of suspense, once said to French filmmaker François Truffaut, "I take pride in the fact that *Psycho* . . . is a film that belongs to filmmakers. . . . The way it was told caused audiences all over the world to become emotional.") Every great movie has its climax scene which remains embedded in people's visual memory.

Usually there is a reason why you remember something, even if it is not always evident; the emotional ingredient is invariably present. Certain details, seemingly without importance, may have personal significance: I remember the day I forgot a pair of socks I had just bought with my husband. Once back at the hotel, I looked for them and then recalled putting them on the floor as I sat in a movie theater. I suddenly burst into a series of self-recriminations, which moved my husband to the point of darting out to find them, reassuring me as he left that I was not to blame and that in any case it was not too late to rectify the situation. The socks were not that important, although they were special—I recall that they were bought at a fine store, hard to find, a fine weave of wool, midcalf length, unusual colors. But what really made an indelible impression on me was how this incident revealed a side of John's character that moved me to tears: Sensitive to the way I felt, he managed to dilute my guilt feelings by sharing the responsibility for this forgetfulness, which he lightly deemed as minor. His pragmatic approach worked. By going back to the theater immediately, he found the parcel exactly where it had been left. He returned with the socks in his hand and a smile on his face, and the day was saved! More important than the socks, I took his kindness and sensitivity as a precious gift. I have totally forgotten which movie we went to see.

The other side of the question of why we remember details rather than the whole concerns observation skills: Through specific training, anyone can learn to distinguish the most important points in a text and remember it with the help of an illustration or example provided by the author or found after reflecting on the subject. An analytical method like the French "Explication de Texte," practiced throughout high school in France, teaches thinking and organizational skills and stresses the importance of personal commentary. The student is asked to analyze the organization of a text, answer specific questions, and highlight the main points and illustrations and discuss them. The purpose of this exercise is to develop analytical and critical skills while setting the mind in the mode of "explaining" (not merely "understanding"). The shift to didactic action, with an emphasis on meaning, vastly improves memorization. (By comparison, the U.S. reading-comprehension exercises I have seen are a pale attempt at finding meaning, because they stop short of the commentary essential to personal meaning—and to memory.) In non-literary areas, essential material is perhaps easier to spot: statistics, facts, identification of objects, percentages, diagrams, etc. Strategies to record these efficiently do exist.

Interpretation of a text may vary, even in the way it is organized. Attempting to eliminate subjective judgments would be an impossible endeavor. Subjectivity will always influence which details we remember, and I think this is for the best; it adds diversity to recollections.

14. Does emotion play a role in attention?

A big role, as illustrated in the previous question. Whether positive or negative, it "seals" and stores the event for long-term recall. We dwell mostly on what moved us, shook us, rattled us, shocked us, pleased us, annoyed us. Emotion sorts out what is important to us. An event that has touched us emotionally is recorded with more depth of processing and elaboration, and leaves the deepest mark in our memory. To verify this statement, just think about unpleasant situations, and you will see that many of them will pop back. You may bring them to life by asking more questions, opening files by categories: work, leisure, travel, people, childhood, home, etc. Employing a network of such associations facilitates recall.

Involuntary memory is especially linked to the mood associated with a subject. For instance, what we learn in a state of joy will come back more easily when we are happy, and what we record in a state of sadness will come back when we are sad. This explains the vicious circle of depression, in which only depressive thoughts spontaneously come to mind. By voluntarily recapturing a certain mood, one can remember episodes recorded in that mood. This "matching of moods" theory has been verified by psychologist Gordon Bower at Stanford University: Students who have learned words under water remember more of them under water than when tested in a room.

On the other hand, emotions can interfere with the attention we should be giving to a primary task. Several years ago, all absorbed in my wedding preparations, I drove away from the florist's shop with my mind still on the flowers, only to be totally startled by the rotating lights of a police car following me. What had I done, unawares? I had crossed a "double-double" line to make a U-turn. I was shocked, furious at the cop, at fate, and at myself (in that order!). In the context of my merry planning, this incident assumed ridiculous proportions in my mind; I even wondered if it might be a bad omen—an absurd idea I immediately rejected as emanating from the natural fears anyone has before embarking on the great journeys of one's life. I can relive the scene, my disproportionate grief, and, most painful of all, having to accept the consequences of my inattention by paying the traffic-violation ticket. Certainly I had excuses as to why I should be forgiven for the infraction, but the law would not hear of them.

This story reminds me of another, about a man who, on learning he had won the lottery, drove through a red light in a state of elation and was killed. The moral: When in the grip of strong emotions, pay double attention to what you are doing, for they prevent you from concentrating on what is objectively most important (here, clearly, the traffic).

15. Does attention diminish with age?

If you say to yourself, "How come I'm so distractible of late? I used to be able to concentrate better than that," you may be right. As we get older, we become more vulnerable to interferences and distractions. That is why it becomes more difficult with age to do several things at the same time with the same degree of efficiency. One tires more easily and gets irritated at not being able to concentrate as well. Many divided-attention tests have revealed that this syndrome grows worse with age. The consequences are often painful: Older people tend to abandon activities that used to give them satisfaction, under the pretext that they cannot do them as well as they used to.

In fact, it is partly a question of organization: One must learn to establish priorities after having renounced "polymorphic activity" (that is, doing several things at the same time). To recall a charming quote by Montaigne: "When I dance, I dance; when I sleep, I sleep." Hail to those who give themselves totally to what they are doing! They enjoy it much more. While it is true that some effects of aging are irreversible, such as the slowing down of metabolism and the greater vulnerability to interferences, it is possible to accept them and modify our behavior ever so slightly, just because it pays off to do so. Either you read or you watch television. Either you concentrate on a cooking recipe or you chat with your friend. By doing one thing at a time you will have the satisfaction of doing it right.

Getting organized boils down to identifying difficulties and finding individual solutions to deal with them. As attention becomes more fragile, you must anticipate situations and prepare for them. By eliminating attention problems, you may have dealt with half of your so-called memory complaints. Integrate the principle of *planting a cue at the time you think of it*. If you suddenly remember, "I must mail this letter and return Mike's book," do both right away; if that's not possible, do something to guarantee that you will not forget when you leave your home: If you group the items in question near your purse or coat, you will not be able to miss them. The weaker your attention, the more you need such strategies. So, get organized:

- act when you think of it—"do it now";
- plant a visual or auditory cue;
- group items;
- do one thing at a time;
- anticipate situations in which attention cannot be sustained.

16. Have there been any studies on attention deficits?

In children, attention deficits have been linked to hyperactivity. In the U.S., the blame for hyperactivity has been pointed at everything from the environment, hard rock music, and caffeine in Cola drinks to parents and that *bête noire*, school, which is so boring, no wonder Junior either yawns or rebels. The fact is that only 4 percent of American children are hyperactive.

Mightn't attention problems rather be related to physical dysfunction? A recent study[2] used the brain-imaging technique of positron-emission-tomography (or "PET") scanning to measure the metabolic activity of the brains of 25 adults, each diagnosed as hyperactive since infancy and each having at least one hyperactive child. Interesting differences between these subjects and the control groups were detected. Not only were the metabolisms of the hyperactive group 8 percent lower, on average, than those of normals, but these metabolic differences were localized in the superior part of the frontal cortex, the

[2] by Dr. Alan Zametkin.

region in the brain regulating attention. The link between the brain's chemistry and behavior was thus confirmed, and so was the hereditary factor.

Still, most people believe that environment plays a significant role in the status of children's attention. A home, loving parents, concerned teachers, a quiet room are all certainly assets. Jane Healy, in her book *Endangered Minds: Why Our Children Don't Think*, argues that television, by manipulating the way the brain responds to rapid changes in perception, can wreak havoc with children's ability to concentrate. Rapid flashes of images and impulsive sounds, Healy writes, reduce the capacity to respond to a stimulus. When the mind is manipulated in this way, thinking rarely intervenes, because certain areas of the brain are preoccupied by the anxiety that is constantly mobilized by a rapid succession of "bangs and crashes." With time, this habit might, according to the author, reduce the vigilance essential to sustain attention.

17. What can be done to eliminate hyperactivity and restore attention?

Until recently, hyperactive children were treated with small doses of stimulants such as methylphenidate, which paradoxically seems to have a calming effect. Coupled with psychological counseling, this treatment has given relatively good results. But the secondary effects of the medications—agitation, insomnia, and arrested physical development—lead doctors to use them with caution. In the adult and elderly population, these medications have given mixed results because of the problem of "tolerance": The body gets addicted to the chemical substance and keeps requiring more to achieve the same result. This addictive effect is unacceptable, not to mention other side-effects relating to blood pressure, appetite, and sleep.

Attention problems in adults may either have their source in infancy or be related to psychosocial disruptions such as lack of interest, isolation, stress, fatigue, and aging. Attention deficits can also be caused by sedatives and other drugs that cause drowsiness. People with such problems often reach for stimulants like coffee or tea in the hope of maintaining alertness; but most of the time they overdo it, and the result is a state of agitation incompatible with attention.

18. Is it true that caffeine and tobacco help concentration?

In small doses, these substances act as stimulants, but in large doses they exert a negative effect on memory. Excess caffeine intake causes irregular heatbeat, nervousness, irritability, agitation—all incompatible with concentration.

Those who say that they cannot concentrate without a cigarette are victims of the work-cigarette association they have rehearsed for so long. This habit, both physical and psychological, proves to be a real handicap, and one with multiple consequences, when you consider the effects of tobacco on the cardiovascular system and the organs—the heart and lungs in particular. Better to resort to fresh air and exercise to stimulate thinking. Walking in particular is beneficial to reflection, as many writers and scientists who have found inspiration on solitary walks in the midst of nature have pointed out.

19. Are there medications to improve attention?

While people can improve their concentration with relaxation and observation training, to this day there is no miracle drug to correct attention deficits.

20. How can attention be improved?

Simply by arousing your curiosity via the techniques of **observation training**. To pay attention is to set feelings and thoughts in motion. By using your sensibility and intelligence, you can guarantee quality recording and recall. The method I recommend follows nature: We perceive the world first with the senses and the emotions; our perceptions are then organized by reasoning. When you are observing something, you are alert and able to concentrate. To grab your attention and turn it into concentration, the subject must be touching or interesting.

You can get actively involved in your observation by asking two basic questions:

1) Do I like it or not? (emotional awareness: What is my reaction?)
2) What is it I like or not? (rational awareness: What causes my reaction?)

This way one develops **selective attention,** the art of focusing on a specific item or set of them.

In my observation training classes, I use 19th-century paintings by Manet, Degas, Renoir, and Monet. I also analyze a series of five 15th-century French tapestries that are quite similar and therefore difficult to differentiate and remember, unless your eye is trained to ignore the overwhelming resemblances and instead focus on the differences.

But of course, you can train on any subject you like. Here we shall examine three prints by M.C. Escher. Let us first see how we can analyze one of the prints in a way that will greatly enhance our recall of the piece. I immediately put selective attention to work as I embark upon my observation with the above two questions in mind: 1) "Do I like it or find it interesting?" (emotional awareness); and 2) "What is it that I like, or that stirs my interest?" (rational awareness).

Initially noting the *mood* of the piece puts you on the path to answering both questions. Is it dark or light, realistic or stylized, straight or humorous? What is it that makes it so?

The first lithograph (See Figure 1) is entitled *Predestination,* a humorous title once we notice the subject: a chain of numerous fish and birds flying and swiming in a complex pattern reminiscent of the recumbent "figure 8" that denotes infinity. (*Visual analogy enhances memory.)* The eye follows the white birds flying in one direction and black fish swimming, with winglike fins, in the other direction—smiling fishes with toothy grins becoming livelier and stranger as they are seen closer up. Their whimsical expression takes on meaning when fish and birds intersect in the middle: To our surprise, as they seem to rush upward toward the center, the fish grabs the bird in its teeth! Humor and emotion grab our attention; we want to look more closely.

We now discover Escher's subtle art of complex reversed patterns: The white-bird-shapes blend into the black, taking on the features of the fish, and vice versa. This metamorphosis occurs along the ribbonlike loop the creatures make as they course across the page. Their graduated sizes suggest perspective and growth. There is movement everywhere. The transformation takes place over many grades of black, white, and gray, and through numerous intermediate shapes. The more you observe and analyze, the more interesting details appear: shapes of wings and fins, eyes and mouths. In spite of the cruel outcome—the black fish (forces of evil?) chomps down on the white bird (forces of goodness?)—there is an uplifting quality to this work. The ambiguity of play vs. serious activity remains to make us ponder, wonder. . . .

After a thorough objective discription, personal comments help us to remember the work in a more personal way. Here is the message *Predestination* conveys to me: "Nothing is what it seems; you never know what to expect; everything, everyone is lamb and lion, black and white (with shades of gray), in constant flux. Life is unpredictable; but if we do not take it too seriously, it is more bearable. Intellectual distance changes the perspective from cruel to whimsical." Incidentally, don't be afraid to interpret what you see, provided you have thoroughly analyzed it first to make sure your comments are justified by what is actually there. Any work of art is open to subjective interpretation, as Escher himself acknowledged in his response to an admirer's

Figure 1. Predestination, 1951.

insistence that she "saw" in one of his prints a strong representa-
tion of reincarnation: "Madam, if that's the way you see it, so
be it!"

(A word of caution: I insist that interpretation and the use of
imagination should come only *after* having thoroughly analyzed
the scene; it is the only way to prevent the projecting of elements
that exist only in the imagination and would distort the real
object one wants to record. To maintain a minimum of objectivity
in observing something, any reflection must be rooted in reality.
By a close analysis of a text or an image, one avoids extrapolation
into fantasy.)

What stands out in this print is action, humor, and above all
the element of surprise. Analyzing it in terms of both objective
and subjective elements, as we have done, will cause us to
remember it for a long time to come. Dynamic and emotional
factors including humor make this particular print more memorable than ones with more-neutral subjects. On the intellectual
level, a systematic analysis focusing on categories such as subject,
composition, mood, etc., leads to more depth of processing.
Observing with the whole self helps us remember more and, as
a bonus, enhances appreciation.

Now, let us see how to distinguish and remember items that
appear very similar at first sight. This exercise is a perfect
example of selective attention: training the mind to select, focus
on, and analyze specific information. When comparing, we must
first acknowledge the similarities and then expend the bulk of
our efforts focusing on the differences. Two prints by Escher
(see Figures 2 and 3) that depict two different landscapes of two
cities are, however, apparently similar in structure. The prints'
striking common elements include rectangular compositions
with fields, houses, and a skyline in the background. I find it
more efficient to first analyze one landscape in detail, then
examine the other for specific differences, rather than jump back
and forth between the two, element by element. I begin by

acknowledging that I like both prints; then I embark upon a search for exactly *what* it is that I like about them. As I proceed, I call up categories such as subject, composition, or mood. Studying Figure 2, *Genazzano, Abruzzi*, I find the mood inviting and mysterious, a bit eery with a dreamlike quality. There is a suggestion of winter cold and silence in the air; a stormy winter landscape. To find out how this mood is conveyed, I look next at the composition: half gardens, half dwellings, with stairways making the transition between the two. Above the rooftops, fluffy clouds both dark and light cover the smooth, horizontal hilltop, against which smoke escapes from the chimneys. The eye is drawn from the front—bare, spindly trees and motley parcels of land separated by shadowy terraces—through roads that seem to turn into staircases as they reach the buildings, to the back, where it comes to rest on the tower's steeple. The middle-lower portion of the print shows intricately designed parcels of land, hilly or in terraces with rows of various trees: some—bare, with delicate frames—in the foreground; others—fluffy, round-shaped evergreens—further away.

Right in the middle of the picture, a row of low horizontal buildings draws a line between fields and city. This row looks to me like a chain of railroad cars attached to a locomotive, with narrow black windows and square flat tops reminiscent of freight trains. (My comment: "A strange mix, with elements of both passenger and freight trains.") The upper-middle portion reveals city buildings huddled together, five- or six-story buildings with painted roofs and narrow, vertical, rectangular, dark windows. Some of the windows are framed in white, others are frameless. The different levels of rooflines suggest a hill, as do the staircases. (I can count six of them, some straight with short steps, others winding or diagonal with long steps.)

Now I look at the light: It is brightest on the roads, the middle buildings, the hill in the background, and the tops of the round clouds. Shades of gray differentiate the buildings and give

Figure 2. Genazzano, Abruzzi, 1929.

Figure 3. The Bridge (Town in Italy), 1930.

definition to the landscape. In dwelling on the contours of the parcels of land, so deeply etched in shadow, and the delicate tree frames, I capture the print's mood, which I now not only feel but understand. Thus I create a strong mental image coated with emotion, the lacquer of long-term memories. The more observant one becomes, the more one discovers interesting details, especially when the work is complex and sophisticated as Escher's is.

Now it's time to compare this print with that shown in Figure 3, *The Bridge (Town in Italy)*. But this time, let's *focus on differences*. I always start with the mood. This print also has a dreamlike quality, but it is more effusive, more cheerful than the other, partly because there is no hint of cold. It is definitely not winter-time. The light is brighter, the plants and trees are lush, the fields in the background flush with crops. The main difference in composition lies in the foreground: steep hills made of large, wall-like rocks on which the town appears suspended and accessible only through a stone-laced curved bridge consisting of narrow steps. Here we have a close-up of rugged boulders, exhuberant bushes, and fancy houses leading the eye toward a promontory overlooking the landscape of fields and town in the background.

The upper half of the picture is another part of the town, which can be reached by staircases—four in all not counting the bridge, all with small steps. After comparing the staircases, I look at the houses: Here the roofs are made of tiles, shown in close-up on the left hill. (In the other print they seemed to be made of slate; the difference in materials corresponds to dif-ferences in the regional residential styles.) There are two churches here, one on the top left and one in the upper-middle center, both flanked with structures overlooking the city, with leafy trees in the middle one and a gazebo-like structure in the left one. The prints' focal points are quite different: In Figure 2, the fields and trees leading toward the huddled, shivering city under a cover of silver-lined clouds; in Figure 3, buildings, rocks, and bushes linked by a staircase bridge spanning an abyss of darkness. The eye lingers on the bridge, its construction, its arch linking two worlds: the wild and the tame, nature and civilization. There is additional contrast between dark precipice and lighted city and rocks.

On careful inspection, it becomes clear that the Escher prints show two different towns, in different areas of Italy, in different seasons, with different lighting conditions. Their common dreamlike quality, stemming from the contrast between the unrealistic, stylized elements and the detailed geometric composition, is characteristic of Escher's work, as illustrated in these three prints. I'll bet that after this detailed observations, you will remember them all, especially if you take a minute to make your own comments—including disagreeing with me if you wish. Take your time and enjoy looking!

Note: To observe well, it helps to have descriptive skills and an inclination to search for specific words to describe what you are looking at. The correlation between memory and vocabulary has been demonstrated in many research studies, including our own, and is easily explained: The search for exact words involves more depth of processing, the set of mental operations that consolidate the memory trace.

Practical application: In everyday life, we tend to have poor recollection of similar things—for example, the castles, churches, and museums that we visit during our trips. Now you can apply the techniques of observation training to help you differentiate them and remember the differences.

The type of structured commentary demonstrated above helps memory. You remember what you note, analyze, and comment on; the more elaboration the better. By contrast, *you will not remember what you have neglected to elaborate on.* The method I teach in my observation-training classes consists of raising questions in a selective manner. First, identify the general impression, the subject, the composition, the colors, the mood. Then, zoom in on details—facial expressions, objects, flora and fauna, their characteristics—using the lenses of interest, emotion, and reflection. As you proceed to analyze the scene, you store the information via categories that will act as prompts at the time of recall. Finally, be sure to indulge in personal comments— what struck you, what you think and feel, the associations that came to your mind while interpreting what you have seen.

If you can integrate visualization at every step of the analysis, and if you review frequently the images in this manner, you will remember. Talking about information is a natural way to review it. Teaching is a marvelous way to continue learning and clarifying one's knowledge, because it requires efforts at selection, analysis, and synthesis.

Observation training is also a course in appreciation: It is through focusing on a subject that one learns to appreciate it. The mere fact of recording particular moments with such intensity, noting revealing details that give character, color, and relief to what you want to remember, allows you in addition to live more fully in the present.

3

Mnemonics: Tricks for Recall

In the previous section, we stressed the importance of paying attention. Now we will outline strategies for improving the three component processes of memory: recording, storage, and recall.

1. Is memory just associations?

Association is indeed the basic process for bringing memories back to consciousness. Memory operates naturally through spontaneous associations, one thing leading to the next with a logical link corresponding to the way the memories were filed; the more they have been elaborated upon by the senses, by emotions, and by personal comments, the easier it is to retrieve them. This is as true of involuntary as of voluntary memory. Almost anything may trigger associations: Conversations abound with digressions brought about by personal associations, such as: "Speaking of glasses, these remind me of the ones I lost while vacationing in Greece. I thought I had completely forgotten them!"

Anyone can resort to various mental strategies to exploit the principle of association. By weaving a large net of voluntary, conscious associations at the time of recording *and* at the time of recall, you widen the context in which each memory is located, increasing the probability of hitting upon a cue that will trigger more memories. *Orchestrating associations is the key to efficient recall.* And this is easily done, since, as the poet Robert Frost wrote, "All thought is a feat of association."

Memories do not happen in a vacuum; There is always something precise triggering them. By looking at a vacation photograph I can revive, if I wish, many memories. In order to trigger associations I describe the contents of the photo to myself, and while doing so, I draw from whatever categories are germane to the photo I have right before my eyes: "Delphi in springtime, trees in bloom, a gorgeous site, but in spite of the sunshine it was bitter cold. Biting northerly winds were swirling in this amphitheater of the gods! Being part of a tour, we found our movements were limited, not allowing for lyrical displays. Our time was monitored; instead of following our rhythm, we followed the guide's. From the pastoral, remote aloofness of this place, we drove back to Athens, a noisy city shaken this particular evening by an earthquake measuring 6.8 on the Richter scale. To come all the way from California, where seismic activity is a constant threat, and then to be shaken up on the 20th floor of a Hilton hotel! The building held up, and my husband and I gathered our strength by jumping in each other's arms. . . . " I will spare you many more details that come to my mind as I relive my trip to Greece. But this sample of associations shows how myriad memories sprang out of a single picture as well as my desire to look at it closely and go beyond the initial association by letting emotions and sensations come to the fore.

We can also learn to use associations to remember things without resorting to feelings or logic, as is the case when we make a knot in our handkerchief as a cue to pick up bread at the store. Mnemonic systems based on non-logical associations have been devised from ancient times to remember faces and names, numbers, or foreign or scientific vocabulary. These are not spontaneous associations, but artificial ones planted at the time of recording and pressed into service at the time of recall.

2. What are mnemonics?

Commonly called "memory aids" or "tricks," mnemonic systems (or simply **mnemonics)** are devices for facilitating recall, which, among the three key memory operations—recording, storage and recall—proves to be the most problematic. Many studies have shown that prompted recall is easy (multiple-choice or true-and-false tests are recognition tests), whereas free recall (fill-in-the-blank or essay) is difficult. By turning free recall into prompted recall, which triggers recognition memory, mnemonics act as insurance against forgetting. Since they are based on the principles of **image-association** and **verbal elaboration,** they involve both visual and verbal memory—a powerful winning combination. In his book on the subject, expert Alain Lieury classifies mnemonics into three categories: codes, cues, and strategies. *All these organizational systems must be applied at the time of recording in order to be effective at the time of recall.* If one plants cues, one finds them easily. For instance, the word HOMES—a cue to memorize the five great lakes of the United States (H = Huron, O = Ontario, M = Michigan, E = Erie, S = Superior)—is only useful if the association was reinforced at the time of learning those names. Grouping words by their first letter facilitates recalling them. This, however, only works provided these new names are also actually learned; otherwise, the cue will prove empty: "HOMES = the Great Lakes, the names of which I did not bother learning" doesn't work. Likewise, if you're wondering why you made that knot in your handkerchief, it shows that the association between the cue and the thing to be remembered was neither emphasized nor rehearsed.

Unfortunately, mnemonic systems are rarely used nowadays. The resistance they sometimes encounter stems from the fact that they are not properly taught. Presented as magic potions, they are seldom analyzed in a way that highlights the processes that make them work so well. One is told to learn this or that without any explanation of how to go about it, which means one is left to one's own resources. Certain people spontaneously use better strategies than others; effective teaching implies giving *everyone* the means to learn appropriate strategies. To effectively introduce mnemonics, one must highlight the principles underlying them (such as image-association—see Question #4, this section—in the systems for remembering faces and names, lists and numbers), and relate them to everyday life. Next they must be presented as a memory game. For dealing with non-logical associations, the playful approach works best. What does it matter if they don't make sense: *Non-logical associations are fun, and they pay off.*

As Alain Lieury points out, the success of mnemonics throughout the ages is probably due to the fact that they are based on natural memory processes. This is why, once demystified, they are accessible to everyone. Like Moliere's *Bourgeois Gentilhomme,* who exudes joy upon learning that he has been talking *prose* all his life, the student of mnemonics discovers that he has always been using visualization and association whenever he remembers the location of an object or place. Then he needs only to extend his ability to visualize an object or place to encompass abstract subjects like numbers, lists, and words. In this manner, he accepts more readily the idea of entering the artificial and weird world of non-logical associations. (There is, for instance, no logical connection between HOMES and the names of the Great Lakes, or between a name and a face.)

The most negative reactions to mnemonics are found among older adults, precisely those who stand to benefit most when they are weaned from logical to non-logical associations. In the "preliminary training" sessions I developed for our research studies at Stanford,[1] people are led through structured, graduated exercises designed to build self-confidence while generating mental image-associations that rely less and less on logic (for example, visualize the following: hand and glove; ship and sea; bottle and sea; hat and sea; pen and sea). In addition, they are taught relaxation techniques for getting rid of anxiety; once this is done, they can better organize their thinking. The results of our research in memory and aging prove that if one does not put the cart (mnemonics) before the horse (image-association and relaxation), older people can successfully learn to use mnemonics and even enjoy doing so, simply because they have experienced how well they work.

3. Is it normal to forget the names of close family or friends?

The more names you have to remember, the harder it is to do. A woman with 23 grandchildren complained bitterly to me because sometimes she would mix up their names. She was genuinely surprised to learn that, given their number and the lack of frequency of their visits, this was normal. Here is a good example of perfectionism, or lack of realism. In general we remember the names that we frequently come across; as for the others, an organized effort is required to bring them back to

---

[1] National Institute of Mental Health grant for studies on age-associated memory impairment at Stanford University, Department of Psychiatry, team of Dr. Jerome Yesavage.

consciousness. Therefore, do not be too harsh on yourself for not immediately remembering the name of a distant relative or former colleague you haven't seen in a while.

If you should stumble on "the tip-of-the-tongue phenomenon" regarding the names of your loved ones, rest assured, it happens to everybody from time to time—although more so to the elderly. With age, accessing words is more difficult because the process is slower and because more words have been stored over the years. Therefore, do not make a mountain out of a molehill; rather, let your "scanner" do its work. Continue talking and be patient: The name *will* make its appearance at its own rhythm. And if it doesn't, forget the incident! It does not mean you are losing your memory. It's just a glitch in the system, which happens at any age.

But if you are really bothered by forgetting names, you can learn a mnemonic system to help recall them as you see the faces that go with them.

4. How does image-association help us remember names and faces?

This question corresponds to people's number-one complaint, at any age. It is especially pressing for Anglo-Saxons, whose language lacks the general greeting so common among Latin languages: Instead of saying "Bonjour, Madame," or "Buenos dias, Señora," they must immediately say "Good morning, Ms. Lapp."

Fortunately there is a simple solution to this problem. To put a name on a face, use a mnemonic based on image-association. At the time of recording, just do the following:

1. Choose **one Prominent Feature** in the face, and analyze it. **(PF = Image #1)**
2. Look for a **Name Transformation (NT = Image #2)** by "listening" to the sound of the name, (or by dividing it analytically into syllables), answering the question: "Does

the name *mean* anything (or make me think of something) *easy to visualize?"*

3. Make an **Image-Association** by visualizing the two together. **(PF+NT)**

For instance, for me you might choose my large, almond-shaped eyes as my Prominent Feature. My surname, LAPP, has several possible associations. Among those, you will do best to *pick the most visually direct one:* LAP, as in "sitting on your lap." ("Lap = distance" is abstract, and "Lapp from Lapland" might convey an image such as a reindeer, which has other connotations—for example, Rudolf or Santa. You wouldn't want to call me that!) Now, once you've found a Prominent Feature and a Name Transformation, you have two images you can combine into an Image-Association. Just visualize the two together—my *eyes* on your *lap*—letting your imagination lead you to some kind of commentary: "How bizarre and surrealistic!" If you want to, you can add a lion to the scene to remember my first name Danielle as in Daniel and the lion's den.

This exercise both forces you to take precise mental pictures in the "close-up" range and develops your imagination. In order to bridge the gap between the name Lapp and the Name Transformation LAP, repeat the name aloud about ten times. In my case there was nothing to it because my name comes so close to meaning something easily visualized, if you disregard the spelling. At the time of recall—upon seeing my face—you will naturally zoom in on the Prominent Feature, which will contain a visual cue via a Name Transformation, "prompting" you to recall my name:

PF+NT (eyes on lap) ➜ LAPP.

The image-association brings you the name on a silver platter. Isn't it wonderful? It is well worth the effort, for, if done properly and rehearsed a few times, it guarantees long-term recall. Even the woman with 23 grandchildren tried it with success (which goes to show that the method also works with first names).

It is up to you to choose your face-and-name image association. Proceed methodically, *one person at a time*. Upon meeting someone in a social situation:

- Choose a Prominent Feature during your conversation.
- At the time of parting, ask the person to repeat her/his name then immediately visualize it scrawled as red graffiti on a white wall.
- As seems practical, go to a place where you can have the privacy necessary to look for a Name Transformation: Ask yourself: "Does the name mean (or sound like) something I can *visualize?*" If the answer is yes, it is easy; If no, it is still possible—you just have to use your imagination. Practice makes a big difference. For example: Fenn = a fin, Brown = a brownie, Grey = the fog, O'Neill = kneeling in front of an egg!
- Do not forget the crucial step: Visualize the two together (PF + NT) while repeating the name.
- Review these faces and names several times during the next week. Strike while the iron is hot, and you will leave a top-quality memory trace.

Now play the game! Good luck to you, and don't be discouraged by a few difficult names; skip them at first, and train with easier ones. The more you think of Name Transformations, the easier and faster you will find them. (Note: This is not a system designed to remember the names of people introduced in a receiving line!)

5. How can image-association help me remember places, brands, titles, foreign words?

The same principle of image-association applies to any type of noun, be it a place, a brand, a title, or a foreign word.

First, find a concrete meaning, or image, in the name; then, visualize that meaningful image together with the object with which it is to be associated. Say you want to remember:

1) the name of a street—*Macarani*, where a bookstore is located. Visualize *macaroni* noodles between the pages of books you are leafing through;

2) the name of a region or park—*Serenghetti* in Africa. Visualize a *syringe* injecting *spaghetti* strands into the thighs of scared gazelles, superimposed on a map of Africa. (The more precise, the better.)

3) the name of a city—*Hokitika* in New Zealand. Visualize a *hockey stick* making a *tick*ing sound on the North West (NW = "New") coast of the Southern Is*land*. (Tip: Adding movement to the image increases the depth of processing, leaving a better memory trace. Try doing it systematically for all image-associations.)

4) the brand name of a product to wash silk—*Princenet*: Visualize *Prince* Charles wearing an impeccable *neat* shirt, the softness of which he touches with delight.

5) the title of a book in association with its author—*Eva Luna by Isabel Allende*. Visualize a Latin Eve = *loony Eva eye*ing the *end* (eye-end = "Allende") of the book before she reads the beginning, or *Eva eye*ing the rear *end* of a loon (but only if you are familiar with this fishing bird; birdwatchers can visualize it easily);

6) the title of a movie or play, in association with its director or actors—(a) Gerard *Depardieu* playing *Cyrano de Bergerac*. Visualize the actor's face with the long nose of the character *depart*ing from the face. (b) Audrey Hepburn starring in *Roman Holiday*. Visualize the young actress on a scooter in front of the celebrated Trevi fountain, staring at her *hip burning*, saying "*OH!*" (Oh for "Audrey," not "Katharine").

Bizarre? Certainly, but efficient for triggering recall. Try it, you'll like it.

6. How can the Loci Method help me memorize *all* my errands?

What could be more frustrating than realizing, once back home, that you have forgotten an errand you very much intended to remember! Most lists of things to do are fairly simple and familiar: "We need bread, chicken, milk, salad, fruit, and cheese, and I must go to the shoemaker and the cleaner's." In spite of this, we often manage to forget some items—unless we use a mental strategy. The most common one consists of grouping objects into categories—dairy products, vegetables, fruits, staples, and miscellaneous errands—in the hope that upon seeing these items on the shelves we will remember. The fact is that the eye has a hard time sustaining attention on numerous shelves filled with merchandise; it jumps from label to label, stopping where the most skillful advertising leads it. Distracted, and often tempted, under these conditions, we buy what we were not looking for, while forgetting what we came in to buy.

Of course, you can always write lists—which themselves may be left at home or lost here or there; in this case you're not using your memory, since you're counting on the piece of paper. Before the advent of the printing press, people used memory systems out of necessity. Even if you still prefer to keep writing lists after learning the following strategy—which ensures recall of *every single item*—try not to use them until *after* you've tested your memory (for instance, while waiting in line at the checking counter) to verify that all items are actually in the cart.

The most efficient strategy for remembering lists, and the least known to the general public, is the Loci method (*loci* means "places" in Latin). Its origin has been traced to a Greek called Simonides, who managed to remember the names of all the guests seated at a huge banquet (which, incidentally, ended tragically when the roof collapsed over the table, killing everyone except our man, who had left earlier). This method for associating place and name was later practiced by the Romans, who found many uses for it, such as remembering the topics of their speeches *in order*. The art of rhetoric implied, to the Romans, not only gifts of delivery and improvisation but a serious strategy for presenting, in a certain order, the points of a discourse covering miscellaneous generally unrelated subjects, as occurs in political speeches. Logic certainly facilitates recall in many cases, but it is useless for bridging abrupt transitions between different topics having nothing in common. Without pen or paper, how could one remember to talk "in the first place" of the *drought*, "in the second place" of *war*, "in the third place" of the *traffic*, etc.? (This is the origin of the idiomatic expression, "in the first place.")

The Loci method responds to the necessity of relying on an artificial order bypassing logic. The key is to establish your own personal list of familiar places that present themselves in a permanent sequence, and can therefore be retraced in order. The Romans for example, used the Forum, the city's marketplace. They imagined taking a mental walk along a certain itinerary, visualizing, for instance, the first place (the butcher's shop); the second, the store next to the butcher (the grocer's); the third place, the next store (the cobbler's); and so on. In each of these places, they visualized "placing" objects associated with or symbolizing the designated topics.

To visualize abstract subjects, it is necessary to find concrete objects or symbols to represent them. For instance: 1) the drought = cracked, thirsty clumps of earth on a quarter of beef hanging on a hook (1 = the butcher's); 2) war = a spear piercing a watermelon (2 = the grocer's); 3) the traffic = a cart running over sandals (3 = the cobbler's). To remember their subjects in order, they had only to mentally retrace their steps through their sequenced itinerary, visualizing these places in which they would then find the cues they had planted. The beauty of image-association is that you cannot see one (i.e., the place) without the other (i.e., the cue to the topic).

You can remember lists of things to do or say by choosing *your living room as a source of from fifteen to twenty loci.* (I gave up on the idea of shopping centers; the stores change too often.) Just itemize the *permanent objects* in your living room, in the order in which they are displayed along the walls. (Ignore the objects in the middle of the room, or mention them last.) Choose different, easy-to-visualize objects for each "place." For instance, going around my living room clockwise, I can describe the furniture and objects as they present themselves in sequence: 1) stereo; 2) cognac leather armchair; 3) Chinese lamp; 4) blue sofa; 5) large painting; 6) green plant; 7) fireplace; etc.) Above all, respect the order in which the objects follow one another. You will then find it easy to retrace them mentally, in sequence. To apply the Loci method at the proper time, you have only to visualize your first item in the first place, your second item in the second place, and so on. These image-associations will remain fresh in your mind for up to 24 hours, after which they will erase themselves like a chalk message on a frequently used blackboard. This "peg" system, in which one literally hangs an object-cue in each place, can be reused over and over again. For those who use it regularly, it constitutes a fabulous aid for medium-term memory: It allows you to retain all kinds of information just long enough to use or write down for later use. Moreover, it will help you to better organize yourself by forcing you to justify the sequence in which you run your errands, which you will group so as to save time, gas, and who knows, even money.

You will notice with pleasure the magic of this method, which can also be practiced as a social game to impress your friends and your children. But before embarking on a stage career, make sure to practice a great deal in order to feel confident about making non-logical image-associations, which proves difficult for those not inclined to use their imagination. By contrast, those who welcome the unusual encounter no resistance—on the contrary. Most people lie somewhere in between these two extremes: At first they do not dare, but once they try the Loci method, they are hooked, simply because *it works!*

P.S. If you know your town well, and if you can visualize different places, you can substitute taking a mental walk past specific landmarks—in Paris, for example, starting from 1) The Arc de Triomphe, going down the left side of the Champs Elysees to 2) the Lido; then reaching 3) the Rond Point des Champs Elysees with its fountains; then 4) the Theatre des Champs Elysees; 5) the American Embassy; 6) the Hotel Crillon; 7) the Arcades of the rue de Rivoli, and so on. This suggestion will appeal to those who are not homebodies. Personally, I find it easier to form mental images of familiar objects found at home because they are more varied and different from one another.

7. How can I memorize instructions or recipes?

To remember instructions and recipes one must isolate the general principles behind them, and visualize an example of each in its particular context. Logic helps retrieve different operations in the order in which they must be performed, if one is experienced in the matter, and it may suffice in examples such as changing a tire, painting a surface, cooking a roast or a fish, making a sauce. But for more complex or less familiar operations, the sequence of the steps to be taken must be written down. When this cannot be done, you can resort to a mnemonic system that allows you to remember a series of items for up to 24 hours.

The Loci method (See Questions #7, this section) is ideal for retaining temporarily all kinds of procedures and how-tos until you can write them down for further reference. In these contexts the sequence is really critical, which is not necessarily the case with things to buy or to say or errands to run. While driving my car and listening to public radio I have had the opportunity to hear all kinds of interesting and expert tips on subjects as diverse as gardening, cooking, health, plumbing, and fishing! With no possibility of jotting down the information, it seems natural to resort to a mnemonic. It also sometimes happens that I witness the making of a wonderful dish at a friend's home, or on television. I promptly proceed to memorize the steps using my Loci. For instance, to make a delicious tuna-curry salad, I visualize in my first place (1 = stereo) some curry mixed with Bulgarian yoghurt + a dollop of low calorie mayonnaise to taste; in my second place (2 = leather armchair) a can of whole tuna fish drained of its water; in my third place (3 = oriental lamp) diced green apples in their skin; in my fourth place (4 = sofa) an equal quantity of diced celery; in my fifth place (5 = large painting) minced scallions or green onions. In my sixth place (6 = green plant), I place all the ingredients in a bowl, which I place into the refrigerator to cool for at least two hours (here, I visualize a big "2" in red on the bowl). I look at my watch and calculate the time it will be ready. That's all. *Bon appetit!*

8. What's the best way to retrieve words?

The "tip-of-the-tongue phenomenon," or difficulty in retrieving words, is a common complaint, one that increases in frequency with age. The more verbal the person, the more he/she is frustrated by it. Most of the time another, similar word appears instead, creating a feeling of frustration in those who like precision.

Studies on the subject reveal that the tip-of-the-tongue phenomenon strikes mostly surnames or names of brands or objects, the first letter of which often comes back alone: "It starts with an R." About half the time, the word comes back in less than a minute. The causes for this temporary loss of access are still unknown: Could it be that the slowing down of metabolism, known to occur under a state of fatigue or in the elderly, plays a role? Or is it a short-circuit of the retrieval system, the most complex memory function? These memory lapses are particularly frustrating because of their unpredictability. They often involve words rarely used (an actor's name, for instance), confirming the difficulty of recalling information without a prompt—a normal occurrence only aggravated by the anxiety it arouses in some people.

Be reassured: Studies have shown that it is normal to stumble over words. Only *relaxation* allows a memory to return to consciousness. You must therefore minimize the importance of such an incident, and learn to go around the obstacle. For the moment, rather than strain to recall the word, use synonyms instead and beat around the bush, continuing to talk about the subject. In so doing, you will trigger associations that will bring back different "files," or contexts, in which this word was registered. As has been verified in several experiments, a word that does not come back in certain circumstances does come back in others.[2] It is worth knowing that to consult memory's library you must be relaxed and confident. Let us admit that sometimes we all have to fumble in the dark for a minute to find the light switch.

The situation is quite different for words over which you stumble repeatedly. You can anticipate them and plant a cue to recall them at the opportune time. For instance, in my living room a large, beautiful plant attracts comments from all guests who notice it. Since I am regularly asked its name *(Anthurium)*, I have anticipated the possibility of forgetting it under the pressure of demand, and planted a cue by making an image-

---

[2] This may be due to the complexity of memory processes. PET-scan research on word recall, led by Dr. Marcus Raichle of Washington University in St. Louis, Missouri, shows that even seeemingly simple tasks "light up" several spots in different parts of the brain at once (not only the speech centers), suggesting that many smaller "processors" or abilities are linked together in complicated networks.

association in the following way: Listening to the sound of the word "anthurium," I look for a concrete meaning in the name. The beginning of the word, "ant-," means a familiar insect anyone can visualize. I let my imagination follow the ant as it climbs up the distinctive tropical flower of the plant, so that I record an image-association linking the two together. When I think about this plant in bloom, I automatically see the ant—the cue for *Anthurium*. Notice the two principles underlying this strategy: a search for meaning (ant), and image-association (ant and flower). These are applicable to many subjects, as you are about to discover. It is up to you to come up with examples and your own image-associations.

A helpful hint to chatty senior citizens: By talking less rapidly and perhaps not so much, you will reduce the number of incidents, since you will use fewer words and give yourself more time to choose, avoid, or retrieve them. And if you become more aware of words through reading, doing crossword puzzles, looking for synonyms, commenting on the vocabulary used in newspapers and on TV, or the "in" words used by the younger crowd, you will notice an improvement in your ability to remember words when you need them. The more consciously you deal with words, the more you revise them and the closer and accessible they are to consciousness. However, the tip-of-the-tongue phenomenon, with its lag in reaction time, is here to stay. You may as well resign yourself to making the most of the situation. My last line on the subject is the last line from Billy Wilder's film *Some like it Hot*: "Nobody's perfect."

9. How come words I can't remember when I need them "pop out" later—often in the middle of the night?

There is no scientific explanation for this delayed reaction. The message has been registered, and the subconscious brings it back to consciousness at random. I have noticed that obsessive-compulsive people complain more about it. Perhaps, although unawares, they continue thinking about their lapse, having more difficulty letting go of the incident because they perceive it as a failure more than others do.

There is, however, a relationship between recall and emotion. When you relax and stop trying to force recall, your "inner scanner" may do its work at its own rhythm. The block disappears, and the word usually comes back within the next few minutes. One may speculate that certain rare words are more difficult to access, and that sleep is an ideal, relaxed state of receptivity where time does not matter. (The very fact that you were upset about forgetting the word may have focused your subconscious on the search.) The words that wake you up have startled you to the point of interrupting sleep or dreams. In the latter case, you will perhaps notice that the dream provided associations provoking the recall. This is rare; but when it happens, the real problem is to forget about the word and go back to sleep!

10. Is there a trick to remembering the spelling of words?

If you pay attention to spelling and learn some strategies, you will remember. People interested in language are often good spellers. They take mental notes of the spelling and make a point of remembering it. They are usually interested in reading and writing, which are natural ways of reviewing words. Therefore, to remember the spelling of words: First, show a modicum of interest in the matter. Second, think about it—supply a meaning to it, or make a comment. Third, write it down on paper, and also mentally spell it aloud and visualize it in red caps against a white wall. Last but not least, *use the word frequently* until the spelling becomes reflex. Once this is achieved, recognition memory will tell you when it is not "right." Writing down several potential spellings, you will quickly recognize the correct one.

As for Step Two, you can find "meaning" through a rational approach or the use of your imagination. The rational approach invokes rules that link a word's meaning to its phonetics or etymology. A good dictionary mentions the latter after the word—for example, "dilapidated," [L. *dilapidatus*]. (If you know Latin, it makes more sense). By highlighting the difference— here *di-*, not *de*—and by rehearsing it mentally and on paper, you commit it to memory. Spelling rules rationalize these nuances. When you know them, you can apply them consciously. Rules are classified in categories: verb-stems, conjugations, double vowels or consonants, and so forth. Unfortunately, the exceptions are numerous; one constantly comes across irregular tenses, plurals, and other syntactic forms. The more knowledge one has, the better.

Spelling rules do help you to remember more easily, because in case of doubt you are able to refer to them; but if you don't know them, or have forgotten them, you must resort to observation and imagination skills, as may already have been the case in memorizing exceptions to the rules. If you are predominantly "verbal," you are naturally more inclined to be observant about words. If not, you will have to find some kind of motivation to justify your efforts at analysis (for instance, "making spelling mistakes reflects negatively on you.")

No matter what your formal education was, simple systematic observation will teach you spelling. Spell the new word aloud and write it down in large capital letters on a board or a piece of paper. Then close your eyes and visualize it in red graffiti on a white wall, spelling each letter. Isolate the difficult part of the word and make a comment if you can: For instance, "Pirazzolo, an Italian name has two Z's like 'pizza'." Double letters are a frequent source of misspellings. Looking for meanings helps recall. The word *efficiency* has two F's: "To be efficient at a task, you must re*double* your *effort*." (Notice that *effort* also has two F's.) Or: "The words *accolade, accord, account* need two C's because they all involve two parties. *Accumulate* needs two because just one will not do; you can't *accumulate* only one thing!" When you start looking for meaning, you will find at least a personal one, and comments will come easily. (Notice how natural it is to repeat the word effectively in the course of making a comment on it.)

Usage determines recall of anything, including the spelling of words. Review them often through reading and writing, and you will remember them well. Jerry Lucas, an unusually brilliant speller, tells of how he started practicing a strategy at an early age out of boredom during long trips in the family car: He would read the billboards on the roadside and *spell all the words forwards and backwards*. This extraordinary training gave extraordinary results. The practice of specific strategies explains success.

A relatively new method of teaching spelling to children consists in showing a series of words written on cards, at regular intervals, every day for a week. Visual, auditory, and kinesthetic memory are mobilized: After the teacher reads the word aloud as it is being shown, the student is asked to read it aloud and then to write it down. The word is then explained and presented in several contexts. This constitutes the **verbal elaboration** so useful to memorization. The results of this strategy for spelling and language acquisition have proved far superior to simply demanding that an incorrectly spelled word be copied a hundred times (or correcting it once and then ignoring it until the next encounter.) Instead of a mechanical activity, a thinking strategy is at work, involving the student at several different levels. Above all, the words are reviewed regularly and discussed. All these steps facilitate the assimilation and integration of vocabulary.

The principle of using the imagination with spelling applies to rules of grammar and their exceptions. Look for amusing comments to explain the unexplainable. In English, for example, "which" is non-restrictive, whereas "that" is restrictive: "The car *that* is in the garage" points out one of many possible cars (the one in the garage), while "the car, *which* is in the garage" refers in passing to the location of the only car in question. In order to remember this difference in usage of the two words, associate "which" with the image of a *witch,* and "that" with the image of the witch's *pointy* black *hat.* Mental speculation helps memory.

11. How can I cultivate foreign languages?

It is difficult to maintain fluency in a foreign language artificially, even when one is motivated. I know this first-hand, having been living in California for twenty years without many opportunities in daily life to use my native French. If you want to prevent the loss of a foreign language—or even your own mother tongue—it is necessary to organize and expose yourself to the language, whether in written or verbal form. Otherwise your active vocabulary will shrink, although you will still maintain passive understanding.

According to your needs or interest, you can either read books and newspapers or listen to radio or tapes. Reading is an excellent way to keep a language in your consciousness. Get some books or magazines on subjects you care about, and read regularly—say, once a week. Books are also available in audio cassette or compact-disk form, which in addition help improve pronunciation. A shortwave radio will allow you to reach many programs in many languages, including your own when you are traveling the four corners of the world. Set a time and place to concentrate on this activity—consistency is a must in language skills as in any other skill. If you find a radio program broadcast in the language you wish to remember, check your local time, and listen to it as often as you can. You may want to take notes or record it on tape for further reference.

Generally speaking, do not miss any opportunity to speak the language, even briefly or superficially. A neighbor, a foreign clerk or student may be your chance to try out your sleepy language. For instance, I've hired a pair of Mexican-Americans to clean my house, and I speak to them in Spanish only. I please a Francophile neighbor by speaking French to her every time I see her. I go and see foreign movies in their original versions, and I try to speak German with a German friend. When I go to an Italian restaurant I exchange a few sentences in Italian with the owner, which amuses us both. In brief, I seize every opportunity to think in the foreign language.

If you have the time and energy, it is profitable to take classes (and even more so, to teach them), if only in a conversational format. In university towns many foreign students would gladly earn some extra income that way. Moreover, adult-education courses are available in the evening or on weekends in many high-school or college programs. Although it is more difficult to start learning a foreign language later in life, the more previous knowledge one has, the more references there are that facilitate new learning. It is starting from scratch that proves most difficult. By recognizing forms common to a family of languages such as Romance, Anglo-Saxon, or Slavic, provided that you know one language well, you need only learn the differences. Armed with a good direct method, you can do very well, especially with a goal in mind—for instance, a trip to Mexico.

Tip: To increase vocabulary actively put the words in context and review them often at regular intervals for several weeks after exposure. (You'll need a minimum of six examples, just as is the case in children's acquisition of their first language.) An amusing exercise consists of combining, in a single-paragraph mini-story, a mix of eight or ten specific new verbs, conjunctions, idiomatic expressions, prepositions and nouns. Ask a teacher or native to correct it, and *review the corrected version several times during the week.* Never rehearse mistakes! Like bad habits, they are difficult to get rid of. At any age it proves easier to learn a good strategy than unlearn a bad one.

No matter what you do, try to maintain contact with the language, and it will come back more readily when needed.

During your first days in the foreign country, you will have to accept the delay in reaction time for words to come back to you. To speed up the process, read in the language during your trip; upon your arrival, turn on the radio or TV. You will thus be exposed to a great deal of words, which will trigger recognition memory. This will give you more self-confidence to speak. I've noticed that by doing just that, I become more fluent faster. To face the world with confidence, there is nothing like organization and relaxation. If you accept your hesitations and fumblings as normal during the first days, you will allow yourself to talk more and retrieve your knowledge sooner.

Keep in mind that the two stages in foreign-language learning—the passive stage of understanding *(recognition)*, and the active stage of speaking and, later, writing *(recall)*—both depend on proficiency, exposure, and above all, practice. Do not blame your memory when these are lacking in your life.

12. How can I best remember what I read?

Do you, like most people, complain of forgetting what you read? First, ask yourself if you are a perfectionist: Does it seem to you that you forget "everything" you read? Define what you mean by "everything." How do you measure your episodes of forget–fulness? Allow me to cross-examine: When the subject arises in a conversation or a discussion, memories from your readings spring back to you, do they not? Rather, the problem is more that it seems impossible for you to speak about them without their being solicited. This is understandable: Two different operations are taking place. **Recognition memory** is easy, whereas **free recall** is not. In complaining about your memory, you notice only the failures of free recall without acknowledging the success of triggered recall.

But I acknowledge your frustration, and so I shall give you tools to eliminate it. First, it is probable that, like most people, you are a passive reader, which explains in part the limitations of your recall. The brain needs conscious direct commands in order to record information accurately. Second, you may not *need* to retain what you read. Without motivation, the mind does not act. The fact is, however, that we are bombarded by information we believe we must swallow. No wonder our memory rebels. To avoid saturation, one must determine what needs to be remembered for how long, and discard the rest. You can always go back to it later. Think of it this way: The advantage of forgetting a text is the joy of rediscovering it.

To better understand why we retain so little of what we read, let us look at the conditions in which we normally read. Reading for pleasure means reading for the moment, without making it a point to retain the information for long term. Today's newspaper replaces yesterday's. When two articles treat the same subject, one completes and echoes the other. Miscellaneous news items remain separate, however, and are rarely recalled by the reading of a parallel item; rather, they simply are replaced in consciousness by other news events of the same type, such as homicides, natural disasters, fighting around the world, medical findings, etc. Usually one does not intend to remember these things either precisely or for long. This kind of reading is very different from the reading done in the context of work or study (although there too, one does not expect miracles from long-term memory).

Paradoxically, it is more difficult to remember what one reads for pleasure, for without motivation, *questioning, commenting,* and *categorizing* do not take place. Above all, you must *want* to remember for a specific reason: *Defining a goal* forces you to *read actively,* something you do not do ordinarily. Instead of reading a text at random, with the vague hope of remembering it, try raising questions *before, during and after* reading. For instance, as soon as I notice an article in my local newspaper on art in San Francisco, I tell myself it would interest my friend Allen, who is writing a dissertation on American art. I ask myself whether it contains new material, or mentions exhibits in San Francisco Bay Area artists, and whether this would be of use to him. I answer all these questions as I read, and later I write a letter mentioning it. (Alternatively, I could talk about it with him over the phone.)

Tip: To focus better on what you read, use your visual memory, as people with superior memories routinely do. The difference will be that you must do it consciously, voluntarily. All descriptive literature lends itself to being visualized, but most other reading matter can also be visualized once you learn how to concretize the abstract by *reading actively through imagery:* Project in your mind pictorial representations of the content of the text. And ask *questions* to tap your analytical and emotional resources. Notice what interests you, and reflect upon it, making mental comments you intend to apply somewhere down the line. All this **depth of processing** contributes to your recording the information efficiently, instead of counting on the miracle of "spontaneous organization," which, in the sense in which it is usually understood, is not there.

It goes without saying that the more motivated you are, the easier it is to do naturally what it takes to remember. But routine, overwork, and aging all diminish motivation, which you must then artificially and voluntarily create anew. Thus, I have made a point of conversing about the news with a friend once a week, which forces me to select the points I have found most interesting. You can do the same thing with newspapers and magazines of your choice. Start by training yourself to summarize an article, to make some form of brief mental comment on it. Comparing several articles on the same subject is challenging for both memory and conversation. You can add TV news programs to provide a visual dimension.[3]

---

[3] In my first book, *Don't Forget! Easy Exercises For a Better Memory at Any Age* , I dedicated a whole chapter to illustrating different methods for serious reading of several types of materials.

If, in spite of all your efforts (but are they organized and efficient?), it seems to you that you forget most of what you read, don't worry: This is normal. Most people are unable to spontaneously summarize an article, especially if they do not have reference files on the subject. They remember only the general idea—for instance, that "it was about applications of laser technology to surgery." (Unless you are knowledgeable in laser technology or surgery, there is too much detail that you cannot put together for lack of a frame of reference.) And, unless they are worried about their memory, most people are satisfied remembering that little; instead of been preoccupied by an article, they turn their attention to another one, and they tend to spend more time on what they know more about. On tests of non-directed reading, measured retention rates are about 20 percent after 24 hours—*unless* a studying strategy is introduced: Summarizing the text and making a comment *immediately* after reading it increases the amount of your recall to 80 percent. For a better memory trace, strike while the iron is hot! Then, review the information at regular intervals during the week following exposure. And finally, use it as often as you can.

13. How can I remember numbers—addresses, floors, measures, hours, flight numbers, prices, temperatures, dosages?

Are there numbers that you remember easily? For instance, birthdays? Do dates have a symbolic meaning for you? Do you do anything special to remember them? (Perhaps you write them down on your appointment calendar, which you consult regularly.) Most people complain of having difficulties remembering numbers, but they typically admit recording some of them quite efficiently. Motivation usually does the trick: Those interested in cars do not miss the numbers of the different models, such as "Mercedes 500" SL or "Peugeot 504," to name just a couple. Those who follow the stock market can relate its daily variations in number form. Those who work and live with statistics quote them all the time.

Personally, probably because I have no natural inclination toward arithmetic, I used to believe I had no memory for numbers—until I realized I had an excellent memory for prices! I have always compared them (training), and I keep an eye on bargains (motivation). I subconsciously trained my visual memory so that I can visualize different labels, often with the original price crossed out and the new price next to it. Visualizing the label, or the number on a building or a page of a book, is the first step to fixing it in the mind's eye. The second step is to make a mental comment highlighting the number: "What a bargain! Only $45 instead of $125, one-third of the original price!" That is enough, when one is motivated. As a male friend used to say in our college days: "I never forget the telephone number of a beautiful girl." Motivation leads us naturally to use organizational strategies that guarantee depth of processing and recall.

By contrast, when motivation is lacking, or when the number is longer, it pays to use mnemonic systems based on non-logical associations. The principle is simple: Just transform the abstract number into a concrete word. There are many codes of associations—visual, verbal, or mixed. Here are my favorites:

1) **The Ten-Picture Code** *to retain short numbers for short term.* With a minimum of imagination, you can picture the symbols behind these numbers:

0 = plate	5 = spread-out hand
1 = spear	6 = serpent
2 = swan	7 = gallows
3 = pitchfork	8 = hourglass
4 = sailboat	9 = snail

To remember the flight number "United 147," visualize the United logo with a spear pointing to a sailboat stopping at the gallows. Some people find this more complicated than the mere visualization of numbers. (The simplest visualization trick is to project a number mentally as red graffiti on a white wall or in neon against a dark sky.) Other people find the game amusing. The fact is that those who are labeled "mnemonists" because of their extraordinary memory do practice these kinds of mental calisthenics.

2) **The Phonetic Numeral Code** is more complex, combining both visual and verbal associations. It is useful *for long-term retention of longer numbers* (e.g., phone, passport, or social-security numbers). Here, each number refers to an image-association suggested by a consonant.

0 = z, s (0 is zero)
1 = t (t looks like 1)
2 = n (n has two bars)
3 = m (m has three bars)
4 = r (r is the last letter in four)
5 = l (L is the sign for 50 in Roman characters)
6 = soft g, j, ch, sh (6 looks like a capital G)
7 = k, hard g, q (k looks like a vertical bar and a 7 inverted
      and rotated counterclockwise)
8 = f, v (in script, f has two loops like 8)
9 = p, b (9 looks like p reversed and b upside down)

To remember a number, just convert it into consonants and use vowels and your imagination to form a cluster of words or a short sentence. (The first association often triggers the next, framing a context easy to remember). For instance, the phone number 258–0639 becomes:

2	5	8		0	6		3	9
n	l	f, v		z, s	j, sh, ch		m	p, b
new leaf				sushi			mop	

3) **Finding Personal Associations** with numbers is another

strategy I especially like, although it is more limited. Simply project your own associations with numbers, reading into them important dates, sizes, heights, ages. It is useful for retaining personal numbers like that of your driver's license, passport, and combination locks, but also for other numbers as well.

Take, for example, the phone number 451–7932. Let us say that you or a loved one happens to be 45 or 51, or that this age means something special (promotion, move, etc.). Start with that and work in an association with the single number: Thus, 4 could be a panty size; 1 = "I am Number One," or a number-one bestselling book, record, movie; 79—could it have been a significant year for you? Think back, perhaps the year of a memorable vacation in Arizona; 32 = another possible real or ideal size of feminine undergarment—yours or your wife's. (Notice how my first association led to this one.) Then put it all together in a sentence: "Moved to California when Joe was 45, he has been named number 1 salesman in his company. In '79 we had a dreadful vacation in Arizona where our suitcase was lost along with all my undergarments. To replace them I could find only the wrong size, 32." Farfetched? Yes, but effective if accepted, reviewed, and personalized. You can group the numbers any way you like.

Here's how I memorized the combination lock of my bike with the help of personal associations: By asking myself, "What do these numbers mean to me?", I came up with this: 43–61—my cousin Robert was born in '43 and my first travel to England was in summer '61. This method works because it uses your own personal associations, provided you rehearse it well at the time of recording and at the time of recall. Try to add visualization and use your imagination: I can see my cousin biking on the English roads near Hastings.

4) **Pure Visualization** suffices to remember a floor, an address, a dosage. *Just visualize the number in large red graffiti on a white wall.* Reinforce the visual trace by making a verbal association:

Add a mental comment using your imagination. For instance, to remember a dosage of five drops per day, visualize five drops falling, one on each finger of your hand (for seven, one for each day of the week). What about a measurement—say, your bed size, 86 by 102 inches? Visualize your bed with these measurements printed on its edge in red. Adding a comment, you may say: "With regular, high-quality sleep, you and your spouse should both make it to age 86 and perhaps over 100— more precisely, 102." Spending a few seconds thinking does the trick. For temperatures, visualize them in larger-than-normal, shiny red numbers on a thermometer and make a comment related to your situation: "42! Over 40° Fahrenheit in the early a.m.! It may heat up even more today, and the snow will melt. What a pity for skiing!"

14. How can I prevent the forgetting of important dates— birthdays, anniversaries, arrivals and departures, special occasions?

The more things you have to do, the more afraid you are of forgetting some of them—and the more you have the impression of doing so. In this case, at least you have an excuse! Sometimes, however, there is none to get you off the hook. Then what are you to do—go consult a psychiatrist to figure out why is it you always forget your wedding anniversary? I propose a cheaper alternative: Use both mental strategies and mechanical reminders. Drop your anxiety about forgetting important dates by getting organized. In the war against forgetfulness, use a battery of weapons:

1) **Anticipation.** *Anticipate the date and make a mental comment* that refers to other events around it (vacations, weekend, concert, hairdresser's or dentist's appointment, visit from so-and-so, "finished that big project," to name a few).

2) **Organization.** *Note the date* on an appointment calendar that you have gotten into *the habit of consulting regularly*, three

times a day, leafing through it several weeks ahead. Make practical arrangements if necessary, specifying and rehearsing the date.

3) **Visualization.** When the date in question comes near, imagine the event, and place a foolproof visual cue in a place you cannot miss: a sticker on the wheel of your car, or in your wallet; a large, colored sheet of paper sticking out of your satchel; or a rubber band tied around your finger. You can also use a timer if you are absorbed in a project and must be out of your office, or home, at a certain time. Do something! Being overconfident about your memory can be as dangerous as lacking confidence, because both lead to inaction. The truth is, only organized action helps in the matter. *Do not assume you will remember—make sure you will.*

4) **The Pause.** Above all, get into the habit of pausing to allow yourself to think and remember. Integrate the pause into your daily life: Ask yourself at regular intervals which are the important events or projects of the day, the week, the month. By reviewing them, you will keep them in mind, which will allow you to remember when the time comes. It is up to you to determine at the outset what is important. From then on, just acknowledge it, and pause now and then. It is not that difficult to regain control of your life by defining your priorities and going after them. If you really want to remember, you will not miss a trick.

15. What's the trick for remembering game scores—cards, sports, etc.?

In order to remember scores, you must appeal to your visual memory. The principle of image-association applies to most things: where you put your personal effects, where you parked your car, where you saw this item or that person, and even scores for various games. With practice, you will be able to visualize the cards thrown down by another player (image-association between, say, a jack of spades and that player's ring, for example); or the position of the players on the tennis court when a particular point was made; or, of course, the scoreboards for ball games (just associate the score with that particular player who scored the point you visualize). Instant replays used on TV can help you review important plays. Image-associations are reinforced by verbal comments uttered as you record the score in your mind: "Good play by Young!" "Why is she throwing away an ace?" This inner monologue is at play, without your being aware of it, whenever you remember something. Do it consciously, systematically, and you will notice a big difference.

Last tip: To count the cards played in a sequence, you can use the Loci method. Visualize the first card played (e.g., the king of clubs) in your first place (e.g., the stereo), the second card in your second place, and so on. (To learn the Loci method, see Question #6, this section.)

16. How can I remember quantities?

Perhaps you have been interrupted while counting spoonfuls of coffee or tea, which forced you to start all over again. Interruptions, whether external (events) or internal (thoughts), break your concentration, especially when you are focusing on numbers registered in your short-term memory for immediate use. Generally speaking, to know exactly what you are doing, develop awareness and observation skills, and avoid at all costs **automatic gestures:** For instance, if you hope to control what you eat, it is essential to control nibbling in front of the television set or while you are working, when your attention is somewhere else. The easiest way to do so, and the wisest, may be to not keep any food around, or at least to measure it in advance. It is possible to organize so that you know the quantities you have swallowed by making it a game to count biscuits, candies, or chocolates each time one enters your mouth. This awareness not only brings along a feeling of control but a superior enjoyment of what you do.

An example: To memorize quantities, say, of ingredients, nothing beats visualization. Just visualize the quantity of water or rice in a measuring cup and pour it in a saucepan, saying to yourself the quantity you are using and "looking" at it in its container. The same is true for spoonfuls. Seeing the amount and commenting on it is more efficient than remembering abstract numbers. That's why you remember a recipe better when you actually watch it being made. This proves true with many other crafts from sewing to woodworking to gardening. By going through the motions, one triggers kinesthetic or "gesture" memory. Verbal comments on these quantities, whether comparisons or calculations of amounts, reinforce the memory trace.

17. What's the secret to remembering dreams?

First, you must really want to remember them (a leitmotif you must be used to hearing by now). Although I often remember my dreams because I find them interesting, the period during which I remembered the most of them in the most detail coincides with my participation in a seminar on dreams. This is understandable, for, following the advice of the psychologist, I had organized my bed table with notepad, pen, and flashlight. Before falling asleep, you must tell yourself, "I want to wake up just at the end of the dream to write it down," which you can do after a few attempts at autosuggestion. I also learned to write down immediately my spontaneous associations stemming from the dream, which are so useful for its interpretation but will be rapidly lost unless written down. As soon as you get into the habit of monitoring your dreams it seems to you that you dream more often.

Everybody dreams (and so do animals—just watch their rapid eye movements and leg twitches, and listen to their moans), but not every dream has the same intensity. Certain dreams are more startling than others, and these leave emotional traces that can often wake you up. To fix them in your consciousness, write them down or talk about them as soon as possible—something that was ritually done at breakfast time in certain primitive civilizations.

A last observation: Studies of REM (rapid eye movements, which occur during dreams) in older subjects show that they dream less often than younger people do, and consequently they have fewer dreams to report. This may be partly due to the decline of spontaneous mental imagery related to aging. However, our studies at Stanford show that the ability to form mental images is a skill that, with practice, can be voluntarily rekindled at any age.

18. How can I remember what people say?

Hearing and *listening* are not the same thing. Hearing is reflex and passive, while listening is voluntary and active. Most of the time we do not listen very well, for we are distracted by our own thoughts. Thus, it is no wonder we remember so little of what people say. This is partly due to the fact that we dismiss much of it as unimportant. Certainly neither every subject nor every speaker is equally interesting. It is up to the individual to resort to selective attention (at play whenever you remember something). To remember what people say, make it a point to select what you are most interested in or what relates to you, and to make a conscious comment on the subject. (In case you're not participating in the discussion, this commentary, which occurs naturally in conversation, can also be simulated through a silent mental monologue.) For instance, because I intend to redo my kitchen, I made a concerted effort to remember what my friend Katherine was saying recently about the renovations in progress at her home. I selected, for future recall, many details which I consolidated by analogy to my projects, imagining how I would feel about the plumbing problems, delivery problems, and inevitable disruption she mentioned. I dwelled on how she handled the incertitudes, the mistakes, how she organized her life, what proved useful to her, what to do and what not to do, and so on. I gave free rein to my emotions and made practical comments in order to retain details that may prove useful to me, such as the brand of kitchen equipment she chose (I visualized the brand name in red neon before writing it on my agenda).

When you want to remember conversations, think in utilitarian terms or in terms of affinities, concentrating exclusively on what is practical or pleasant. This selection may seem narrow and egoistic, but it will prove to you that your memory works well when personal involvement and affect are present. You may become aware of the kinds of things you consider important or unimportant. When the context is your work, the emotional factor will manifest itself in your desire to improve your skills: Anticipate how you might use the information and the effect it might exert on your performance.

Other practical tips: First, make sure your hearing has not deteriorated without your being aware of it. If you cannot hear properly, you do not record properly, yet you blame memory for the perception deficit—a common error of older people and others who minimize their hearing problems. The main reason you do not remember, however, is usually not your lack of hearing, but rather your failure to listen or pay attention. Rare are those who listen carefully with a receptive attitude and a concentration that guarantees recall of what others say. It is not always easy to admit that one is bored or irritated by people's conversation, because it forces one to acknowledge in oneself a certain impatience or lack of receptivity. Without a minimum of interest, attention cannot be sustained. Fortunately, the art of listening can be cultivated. Curiosity and the desire to learn and communicate play important roles in effective listening. Indeed, personality factors must be taken into account. Those who are interested in others and want to show their sympathy often listen with more attention than do narcissists or anxious persons preoccupied by their own response to the words they have heard; the attention of the latter is scattered, hence less focused. (But then, let us admit that the world is divided into two species: those who talk and those who listen, the extroverts and the introverts.)

It is also obvious that you will concentrate better if you avoid distractions—which is not easy in a social situation, especially when several people are speaking at the same time. Get your ear closer to the person whom you want to hear talking, and fix your sight on a neutral object: a blank wall, say, or the floor. This is a must at parties where there are many people milling about and a brouhaha in the background.

A useful technique for remembering what has been said is to *rephrase it immediately in the form of a question or a comment.* This forces the mind to summarize and extract the main points, and is particularly useful when a possible ambiguity is present: It is during the conversation that clarification must be achieved to make sure you record what is actually said, and not what you want or expect to hear. For instance: "I am delighted about the good news! Did you say you have set a date for the wedding next summer?" Do not hesitate to rephrase what is important, for it shows your interest and turns you into an active listener. People will notice it and appreciate it.

In a classic study on listening, subjects of all ages and walks of life were tested on recall of a newspaper article that was read to them. They were told they had to remember the article's content in order to discuss it in a group immediately afterwards. Their comments were recorded on tape, and they were later to restate who said what. The results proved interesting: Young and old remembered well the content of their reading, as well as what they themselves said. But older people had more difficulty recalling what others said—which, let's face it, may be a lesser evil since you can always ask another person to repeat it. Forgetting what you yourself have said would certainly be more annoying. (Come to think of it, there is no good liar with a bad memory.)

19. How can I remember sounds and colors?

Both instinct and strategy are helpful in the recording of sensory material. Whereas instinct is spontaneous and vague, strategy is rational and can be analyzed. It has been said that from early childhood, Mozart could memorize and reproduce a piece of music after having heard it only once. The genius of this child prodigy, who took the music world by surprise, defied any explanation. How did he do it? Since he learned to read music and started composing almost simultaneously, we can assume he visualized the sounds on the musical staff as well as on the keyboard, and mentally recreated the notes of the melody. He used to play a piece immediately after hearing it, which is not only most impressive to an audience, but also crystallizes the memory when the trace is at its freshest. Musicians are known to have an exceptional memory for sounds, although few of them to that degree. They mentally "hear" whole pieces of music, so that they can rehearse anywhere, even far away from their instruments or orchestra. The same is true of exceptional athletes, who are able to rehearse their training through visualization. In addition, some people have a natural memory for sounds and colors. Most of them use these capacities in their professional lives or in their hobbies, even if only to whistle a song just heard over the radio, which serves as practice.

In fact, the notion of giftedness is difficult to disassociate from that practice. True, one must recognize in virtuosi exceptional aptitudes that have no direct relation to conscious method or training. However, strategies underlying what these master do can be highlighted and taught to help others imitate the underlying memory skill. Here, selective attention takes the form of an ability to concentrate on a decomposable harmony of sounds, colors, motions, and so forth. The principle is the same in each case: *Concentrate on the sensation, analyze it, and dwell on it.* Let us take an example that is practical in everyday life: We often have to remember colors, for reasons ranging from the simple need to find our car in a large parking lot to the decision to match clothes, accessories, upholstery, linen, or to remember places, art exhibits, and more. Studying a color chart is a good way to begin analyzing colors. Beyond the basic colors of the rainbow, there is a scale of tones and values within each primary or secondary color. Whether dark or light, warm or cold, shiny or matte, bright or dull, a color is, in reality, typically made of several colors. For instance, a green may verge on yellow or on blue, a red may verge on orange or on purple. The more you analyze (and verbalize by commenting), the better you will recall. You will be able to describe to a salesperson the color you are looking for, and to recognize it when you see it.

Another way of fixing colors in your memory is by associating them with familiar objects such as "the blue in my bathing suit," or with more general points of reference: "pine green, salmon pink, Chinese red." Artists and art students buying paints know that colors have names, but anyone can visualize them if he/she refers to something well known, such as salmon flesh or red Chinese decorations. Visualize intensely the color you want to memorize. By doing so, you will develop your visual memory and will recognize colors more accurately.

Likewise, when hearing a piece of music, study in particular the transitions between movements, because they act as cues for what is to follow. Each musical sentence is made of notes and rhythms that can be linked together through analysis and, above all, practice. By rehearsing those links, you strengthen the associations between musical elements.

The more you expose yourself to colors and sounds—the more you observe, review, and *think* about them—the better you will remember them.

20. How can one prompt recall on a specific subject?

Whether it is people, places, or themes you are trying to bring back to memory, your best bet is the "question game." To provoke recall, just ask general or specific questions that will trigger associations through **categories**. There are many kinds of categories—emotional, sensory, or intellectual. Categories may refer to mood, the five senses, or diverse subjects. The miracle of involuntary memory proves that one can resuscitate memories from associated stimuli. A pale, frosty streetlight brings me back to a small Austrian village where, one night, I was walking back home after dancing. I was 20 years old. Associating, I can see the frozen river, feel the icy air on my humid brow, hear the snow creaking under my boots. The more I dwell on these sensations, the more details I accumulate. The cold air reminds me of the German tradition of sleeping with the windows open, even in the winter. I used to wake up with a frozen nose!

Notice that the first sensation is only the starting point for the domino effect of recall. Afterwards more memories can be triggered by calling up various categories. The rebuilding of memories is a creative endeavor. By way of analogy, the French poet Valery demystified poetic inspiration by pointing out that a single verse, no matter how beautiful, does not constitute a poem. The rest—that is, constructing the entire poem—is the poet's craft.

When dealing with a precise subject, ask yourself precise questions. Following the preceding example, I ask about this period in my life, my first love, our vacations in the snow: pleasures, sport, meals, outings, joys, frustrations. Within each category, several details come back to me. When I am satisfied, I stop digging. You will see that it is sometimes difficult to stop the rush of associations flowing back to consciousness after opening up categories. In a more intellectual context, you may resort to logical deduction, but also to visualization. To remember Descartes' rationalist theory, consider the image of wax or of a stick in the water, from which the great philosopher's reasoning can be reconstituted: In search of truth, beware of perception and trust reason. The stick may seem broken, but it is not; it is an optical illusion. And wax appears liquid or solid depending on its temperature, yet it is one and the same substance. Therefore, beware of perception, which might lead you astray, and trust reason, its superior.

To prompt recall, it is essential that you give yourself time to organize your thinking. By raising questions, you open categories in which a gold mine of information has been registered. The more you think about a subject, the more you will unveil details you might have thought gone forever; you are thereby placing yourself in a situation of **recognition**, an easy type of memory facilitated by a cue. If nothing comes back when you attempt to call it up, it is probable that nothing was registered, for various reasons: lack of motivation, perhaps, or of attention, or organization. Do not get hung up on it; switch to another question instead.

Keep in mind that without elaboration at the time of recording, the trace will be fragile and may be erased with time. Only cumulative learning allows integration of new elements. The best thing to do is learn a little every day, think about and sift through the material, reviewing it several times in different contexts, rather than cram the day before the exam. Rote learning and pure repetition pay off for the short term only, and then only if the mind is rested. When this is not the case, memory fails; you are not able to use the information thus recorded to write an essay or do a synthesis. Important: The night before an exam, interview, or lecture, make sure you rest and allow your mind a good night sleep.

21. What's the best way to remember messages?

To remember messages for or from parents, colleagues, or friends, you must give them some importance. Having assumed responsibility for transmitting a message, you must organize to make sure you don't forget. The reason one so often does forget has to do with motivation and personality. Some dreamers do not make any effort to remember, thinking that their nature renders them unable to do so and that people will forgive them (which usually happens!). Adverse consequences of forgetting, on the other hand, motivate us to act. Secretaries jot down messages in an efficient manner. Every one of us can use their technique: Name, date and hour, subject, and phone number written down on a note block near the telephone (or these days, entered on a computer). Use your pocket appointment book for writing down messages, and review them several times per day. Keep them in mind until you have acted upon them. Just thinking about the event now and then, anticipating and visualizing it, will make a difference, you'll see.

Get into the habit of pausing before you go anywhere. It will allow you to gather your wits instead of rushing into your next activity. Ask yourself questions: "Where am I going? Whom am I meeting? Did I need to bring something? Are there any messages to relay? Did I check all my messages on the answering machine? Must I go by the office? Is there enough gas in the car? Should I buy something for dinner? There was something I had to get . . . Let us see if I can remember it: What was I doing this morning? I was putting my winter clothes away and—I needed moth spray to protect them! I *got* it!"

22. Does taking notes help? Why do I forget ideas unless I write them down?

It's easy to forget ideas when they have not been integrated into a context. The more you've pondered a subject, the easier it will be to integrate new increments of information, making them more accessible to recall. In the meantime, it's wise to write down new or undeveloped ideas, which is no news to creative people—writers, journalists, lawyers, and other professionals.

Should you "lose" an idea, don't worry, it's only temporary; the thought came to you by thinking of the subject, and it will come back the same way. Ignore the incident and continue working as usual. Above all, avoid blaming yourself for a natural phenomenon that happens to anyone. Your anxiety and your worry will only defer the idea's return. By concentrating on the subject you will touch areas likely to trigger recall. React as you would to a garbled message on your answering machine: If it is important, it will call again.

I am often asked whether taking notes helps memory. Certainly visual memory is involved in writing, but under which conditions? If you take notes carefully, thinking about their content, and if you review them several times, the answer is yes. But if you are in the habit of jotting down copious notes mechanically, the answer is no. In the context of work, it is easy to see that not everyone takes notes with the same degree of proficiency. Those who take useful notes are those who know how to summarize and zoom in on the essential. Most of us try to write down everything, and therefore we fail to listen carefully. When we review our notes, we have difficulty interpreting them. In these circumstances, taking notes proves useless and may even be detrimental, since it interferes with attention. Moreover, we must take into account the following psychological factor: Once you write a note, you may not do anything else, instead counting on your note—a crutch that often crumbles just when it is needed.

You can learn to live without little notes scattered all over the place, simply by using them sparingly. This forces you to prioritize and evaluate the conditions in which you forget. You can and should anticipate the situations in which you will be in a hurry, interrupted, or agitated. Anticipate these situations by grouping objects to take along with you when you rush off and putting one single note on the door or your satchel. Using multiple scraps of paper reveals lack of self-confidence, as well as lack of a better strategy to recall information. By covering your desk or your refrigerator door with little notes, you defeat your purpose, since no single note can attract your attention.

To reduce the use of paper stickers, you can learn to take mental notes with the Loci method (See Question #6, this section). This method functions as a mental notebook, each page being discarded as soon as the information on it has been used.

Rather than rely on bits of paper, which often get lost or misplaced, use your mental resources: your willingness to remember; your conscious awareness; and your visual memory, by taking mental pictures of what you want to record. Thanks to the zoom lens of selective attention, you can concentrate on the essential, which you should analyze in detail. If you make a comment—especially one reflecting emotional involvement—on something, you will record it as a priority. To make it stand out as important or urgent, visualize a red flag beside it. Try following these precepts, and be confident. You will quickly notice the difference. The more you use your brain, the sooner your paper notes will become obsolete.

23. How can I remember appointments?

First, sort out your obligations and establish priorities. Do you remember important work-related appointments? personal appointments? Do you have too many things to do? If you suffer from overload, as so many of us do, one episode of forgetfulness is no big deal. What kind of appointments do you tend to miss? Would you say those you want to avoid? If so, ask yourself whether you couldn't have refused them in the first place. Some people, too shy or too kind, think they cannot say no. They allow others to overwhelm them with demands that many others would not accept. Overwork and overload affect memory.

If you do not find a pattern to your forgetfulness, the problem may be simply a matter of poor organization. Do you own a pocket appointment book? Do you write your appointments in it? Above all, do you consult it regularly, at least three times a day? Do you keep it up to date, crossing out what has been taken care of? Do you write down important information about the people you are going to meet—name, phone number, subject, affiliation, meeting place? Do you spend a few seconds thinking about it, imagining and anticipating your meeting? Do you often pause and reflect, asking yourself if you were not supposed to do something special this morning? Do you play "the guessing game" to trigger recall? "Could it be an errand involving my wife? my car? a dinner party? Could it be something to pick up—laundry, my shoes, photos?" Probably you do none of the above. No wonder you miss appointments, if you do so little to make sure you remember them.

As a last resort, a sticker helps in certain cases. For instance, to remind you, as you leave the office, to go to the dentist instead of going directly home, plant a cue: Place a sticker on the inside of your car window, on the steering wheel, or on your satchel. Efficient people give their memory a head start with good organization. Once planting cues becomes second nature, memory—and life—will be enhanced.

24. How can I avoid losing the thread of my thought, or land on my feet, in case an interruption should occur?

Losing the thread of one's thought can happen to anyone at any stage in life, but the frequency of such episodes increases with age, because one becomes more vulnerable to interferences. The best solution is to prevent them, which is possible much of the time.

In an earlier section, we mentioned "exterior" interruptions such as the telephone, the number-one enemy of those who try to concentrate on their work. Instead of darting to grab it as it rings, finish what you were doing or plant a cue that will enable you to return to your task immediately after the interruption.

Set some rules to protect your concentration. When you are working, you deserve some consideration. A sign on the door—serious ("Please do NOT disturb"), or humorous ("Silence, artist at work!")—could do the trick. Colleagues or children will respect your priorities and will interrupt you only when it is urgent. This will force them to take more initiative, which will free you. If you work in a noisy environment, use earplugs.

Alas, "interior" interruptions are even more difficult to control, and cannot always be avoided. During a conversation, for instance, when an intruding notion or emotion makes you lose the thread of your thought, and you forget what you were saying, what are you to do? Above all, do not panic! Instead of getting upset, keep your cool, acknowledging that such incidents happen to anyone at any age, and that your anxiety will only make matters worse. You have a choice of two strategies: You can either continue talking, or you can let others talk, which gives you time to retrace the conversation. Think about your opinion on the matter under discussion. The lost idea is probably related to it and should come back in time for you to use it in the interaction. In case it does not, just drop it without feeling bad about it. If it was important to you, it will come back when the context arises. If not, goodbye!

The digression, a special type of interruption, is semivoluntary. The relationship to the subject being spontaneous and subjective, it is more difficult to retrace through logic. Psychologist B.F. Skinner, addressing an audience of elderly intellectuals, once made the following recommendation to prevent the loss of one's thread of thought when making a presentation: *"Do not digress!"* He is certainly right, but personally I think it is a pity to eliminate all digressions, because they often bring a change of pace and interesting anecdotes. I think you can indulge them if you organize so that you will land on your feet. If you're reading notes, put a mark where you stopped. Or tell the audience you are digressing, which involves them in remembering what led to it.

Accepting help from others may make you appear more human and bring you closer to your audience; moreover, the mere fact that you've made the point may be enough to help you remember later on where you were. Another more sophisticated strategy is to use the famous and powerful Loci method described in detail in Question #6 of this section: Just visualize a symbol of the subject preceding the digression in your "first place." Say I were talking about my writing a book: I would visualize my book on my stereo. To recapture my thread of thought all I have to do is visualize my first place, and I will find what I mentally placed there. Image-association works wonders in guaranteeing recall.

Finally, realize that the logical link is not indispensable to holding the interest of an audience! In case you do not find your lost idea, tell yourself that your listeners may have forgotten it, too. It is up to you to redirect their attention to something else. A good lecturer or actor does that instinctively. Dale Carnegie insists on three important points to build confidence in public speaking: First, people who come to listen to you are receptive to what you are going to say. (You have the advantage, since you know something they do not, otherwise they would not be there. You are the expert.) Second, you have something to say and you know your subject. (Otherwise *you* should not be there.) Third, you are the only one who knows what you intend to say. You can always change your plans according to the circumstances.

Therefore, no matter what, do not lose your cool. Keep on talking! No one need ever notice your lapses. The art of improvisation, like that of relaxation, must be cultivated. Both work wonders for memory.

25. How do actors remember their lines?

This seems to be an irrelevant question to actors and those who direct them. It is as if memory was a kind of internal breathing at work unconsciously since early childhood. (At school the question is not formally raised either. Students are just expected to learn, not specifically taught how to learn. It is up to the individual student and the teacher to come up with memorization strategies.)

Among the problems actors face, memorization seems to be the last on the list, if one goes by the literature on actor's preparation. The only reference to memory I have ever seen was to *affective memory*, used in the Stanislavski method as taught by Lee Strasberg of the Actor's Studio in New York: In order to get into the role of the character, the actor (or actress) must identify the emotion of the situation and search his memory for an incident in which he felt the same emotion. By reaching into his reservoir of life experiences, the actor enriches the artificial scene with real emotions resuscitated for the occasion. Instead of pretending to feel the emotion, he actually feels it thanks to this return to his past, which adds intensity and a ring of truth to his interpretation. (Among male actors, James Dean and Marlon Brando best illustrate the Studio's method.) Rather than help actor remember the lines, this method aims at liberating him from the words so that he can concentrate on the emotion, the objects, the mood of the scene, and body language. Paradoxically, words will come naturally if immersed in their emotional context.

Stella Adler, whose method opposes Strasberg's, proceeds from the script, which she reveres as she does artificial diction. You would think that she would give tips to recall the lines, but she does not. Again, it is as if memorization just happened naturally: Nobody dares complain, nobody bothers giving tips to help recall. Probably those who do not trust their memory do not choose this profession. But what do actors do to memorize their lines? Could their manner of preparation highlight the memory process they go through?

Researching the subject, I came across a book by Foster Hirsch, who retraces the history of the Actor's Studio. I isolated several elements of actors' preparation that contribute to leaving a good memory trace:

1) *Emotion*. Dramatized emotion is perhaps even stronger than regular emotion, which proves so efficient to fix memories in everyday life. Whether he resorts to his affective memory or to his imagination, the actor spends a considerable amount of time living (experiencing) this emotion through words he rehearses over and over again. Emotion helps seal the lines into memory.

2) *Personalization*. The actor makes this emotion "his," by borrowing from his own past. (We remember better what is personal, because it has gone through a process of elaboration.)

3) *Gestures, speech,* and the other languages of the senses. These involve different types of memory—visual, verbal (auditory), olfactory, and kinesthetic—which are all complementary and reinforce the memory trace.

4) *Analysis.* Studying a script, whether alone or in a group, facilitates memorization of transitions and cues.

5) *Cues.* These are carefully pointed out and rehearsed.

6) *Repetition* of the script and numerous group rehearsals. These help integrate all the above elements.

The famed Stanislavski method is based on awareness and relaxation, the foundation of memory training. Once relaxed and confident, the actor can focus on the emotion, the object, the gesture, the cues; and he rehearses the scene so many times that it gets etched in his memory. The character becomes a second skin he can slip on easily as long as he is playing this role. As a director of the American Ballet Company once put it: "When movement becomes reflex, the battle is won."

When an actor feels he can become his character, borrowing his words, the fear of forgetting disappears. And what about the possible memory lapses no one is immune to? The technique of improvisation will take care of them, making them unnoticeable to the audience. For a better performance, laugh off these rare episodes, which every actor learns to hide.

The actor's prodigious memory is demystified when one understands that lines are much more than words. Preparation for a role records the scene on different levels; it has been widely recognized for centuries that rhyme, rhythm, tune, and metaphor make poetry and song easier to memorize verbatim than prose. (Aren't there some poems learned in childhood that still linger in your mind?) It is interesting to notice that actors' memories function in the same way as anyone else's memory in the areas he/she is interested in. Whenever fear of forgetting is present, anxiety flares up and handicaps memory, as occurs in stage fright. But whenever you are relaxed and confident you can focus on efficient strategies to fix or retrieve a memory trace. This is done naturally, seemingly without effort—at least up to a certain age which varies from person to person. Katharine Hepburn, Spencer Tracy, Jessica Tandy, to name a few, continue to astonish us with their brilliant performances in their twilight years.

26. What are the strategies for increasing work efficiency?

Organization is the key to good memory management. When the following principles are used, recall is made easy. Make sure you *do these things consciously* at the time of recording the information:

Anticipate what must be remembered and take steps to plant cues for later recall. Exterior aids like stickers should be used sparingly. Learn to rely on interior aids—that is, mental devices such as the Loci method—to remember important things to do or to say.

Review information several times before meetings, and you will command your subject without fear of forgetting. Review information *immediately* after you have been exposed to it: You will record it better.

Prioritize and rehearse mentally several times a day what must not be forgotten. To heighten your concentration, try doing one thing at a time.

Follow through and make sure your employees or coworkers do too. Examples: checking a reference and inserting it where it should be; calling a client who is waiting for information; making sure an urgent letter has been mailed and has arrived on time, that a paycheck was cashed, etc.

Delegate lesser tasks; you will have less to remember and thus will be able to concentrate on matters more important to you. This is intelligent selective attention at your memory's service, preventing overload. (Acknowledge and reward coworkers for remembering to follow through on your requests. In so doing, you will convey the importance of memory in the workplace.)

Do it now! Do not procrastinate! By dealing with urgent matters when you think of it or when they present themselves, you get rid of them right away, thus freeing your mind and preventing potential forgetfulness.

Check and double-check important matters immediately and at the end of the day. (This includes items you have delegated to others.)

Use your pocket appointment book more efficiently by writing down names together with affiliations, subjects, and phone numbers; you will thus have all the information you need at your fingertips at any time. Consult your book three times a day, looking carefully at the daily appointments, dwelling a second or two on each, and making a comment if you can. Glance at the whole week once a day to anticipate and review what is coming.

Make it a point to remember information about people—especially details that when recalled, will show your thoughtfulness: their likes and dislikes, their opinions on subjects, and what you have in common with them (family life, fishing, skiing, wine, traveling). Show interest by asking questions; this will help both your social interactions and your memory.

Take brief notes on small cards you can carry in your pocket, during meetings, business lunches, trips.

Be actively involved: Discuss, comment, rephrase what people say. If you get emotionally involved you will remember even better. Above all do not sit passively, unconcerned. Reaction and specific action help memory.

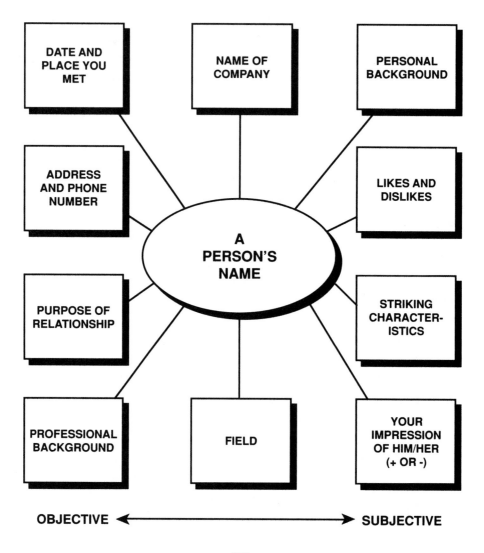

27. What memory strategies can we teach our children?

The age at which specific strategies should be introduced is controversial, since a child may be able to learn a strategy sooner, but not be able to integrate it and use it spontaneously until much later. Flexibility in using strategies and applying them to different contexts increases with age. However, it is my belief that, taking into account the major stages of development and wide individual differences, parents can coach their children to help them focus their frail attention and develop their observation skills. First, children can be encouraged to make a point of remembering, to assume responsibility for recording information correctly. Next, they can be shown how to actively use external cues such as grouping "to take with me" objects together or writing reminder notes, as well as internal cues: searching for meaning, establishing relations (looking for resemblances and differences), rehearsing, visualizing, making comments on whatever they must remember. Specific strategies can be introduced for specific tasks like reading or writing by showing how to think in terms of categories, grouping, and organizing. For instance, adolescents should be taught the strategies used by highly efficient adult readers:

To summarize: 1) Delete or ignore trivial information (younger children must be taught which information is trivial). 2) Reword terms (or paraphrase in your own words). 3) Select a topic sentence, or invent one. 4) Combine paragraphs.

To review a text: 1) Restate its contents. 2) Backtrack and reread unclear points. 3) Look for information complementing the text (personal associations with other material). 4) Use problem solving (asking questions and using dictionaries and discussing ideas with others to resolve difficulties in the text).

It takes years of practice until selective attention becomes a well-tuned spontaneous behavior in adolescence and adulthood. Selective attention is the key to concentration, the prerequisite to good memory performance. Among normal children, learning disabilities are often due to poor attention.

Encouragement, praise, and the rewarding of a child every time he/she remembers something makes the behavior more likely to continue, provided it is demonstrated with success over and over again. If you are patient and don't place your stakes too high, neither you nor the child will be disappointed. It is wise to *avoid punishment at all costs,* since it is so hard to pinpoint the stage in development of a child, some being more shy or introverted than others. All you can do is offer the bait; the child will take it when he/she is ready. If this is done with material the child is interested in, it becomes a game, and your goal is won. For instance, observation training can be practiced anytime, anyplace, by pointing at things and analyzing them. Guessing games can be devised to discover items such as a name or a drawing hidden in the decoration of a cake covered with almonds or beads. Arousing curiosity is the key to spontaneous observation.

28. What can I do to make a memorable impression?

Some people have striking physiques, strong personalities, unusual voices, a style of their own, mannerisms that somehow stick in memory. They naturally attract attention because they are *different.* Anyone can make the most of the principle of differentiation. To be noticed and remembered, *do something* to draw attention to you, your skills, and your ideas. Here are a few pointers:

Try doing things that others do not think of doing, or would not do, extending yourself to be kinder, more interested, more active; taking initiatives; and showing that you care—for instance, writing a thank-you note to someone who gave a seminar for your company, or sending a postcard to clients or colleagues. Using the phone also helps you keep in touch, as the phone companies like to remind us. Use these pointers and you will be remembered.

Make personal connections, drawing attention to what you have in common, and then discussing it. For instance: "This sales representative likes boating in the Sacramento delta. I like boating too."

Be a good active listener and get people to talk about what you both are interested in. Be sensitive to what others say, and comment on it. Few people show genuine interest. Your enthusiasm will set the stage for further contacts. If you initiate them, always *follow through* with them. Since this behavior is rare, you will stand out and be remembered.

Participate actively in discussions and conversations rather than withdraw and just sit there.

Emotions, humor, metaphors, jokes—the unexpected—leave a better memory trace than neutral stimuli. Use this to your advantage in any context where you wish to leave a memorable impression.

Make eye contact and repeat your name as you give your business card when saying goodbye.

Through action, you will become memorable; as the saying goes, "actions speak louder than words" and stick better in memory because they touch our lives.

29. What are the principles of good retention?

The answer to this question constitutes both a synthesis and a review of the material in this book. Here are the principles of good retention: Integrate them into your daily life as good habits that will facilitate memory while improving your attention, your concentration, and your organization.

Pause. Making the pause part of your daily life will give you time to react to your surroundings and to think. Keep in mind that memory is mostly thinking strategies. The pause controls the tendency to rush, thereby harnessing attention. It also fights distractions and interferences. It is the prerequisite of observation. Before leaving a car or a place, *pause* and look around: You will not leave anything behind.

Relaxation allows you to discard anxiety, which interferes with attention or blocks the recall circuits with negative worries or inefficient thoughts. By practicing this mental hygiene, you will feel less tense and therefore more relaxed. You will record more information more accurately, and you will recall it more easily. Whenever you get nervous or upset because you cannot recall your errands, calm yourself down by breathing deeply, and give yourself time to think of ways to prompt recall: Try *observation*—just look around you; *categories*—itemize things to do, places to go, responsibilities, etc.; *questions*—the guessing game (See Question #23, this section) is fun, and often pays off.

Awareness is the key to **selective attention** and **observation**. There can be no guaranteed recall without them. First, and foremost, maintain sensory awareness: Use as many senses as you can in order to record what interests you. Try to perceive the world the way children do, and you will be surprised at what you were missing. Few people are very observant, yet they blame their memory for their lack of attention. By taking mental notes of more significant details and cues, you will not only better remember people, places, directions and important matters, but you will appreciate your environment more. Just stick to the "golden rule" of depth of processing: *Select, Focus,* and *Analyze.*

Image-association (*visual* elaboration) is an essential principle used by everyone who remembers where something is: glasses on the desk, keys next to the telephone, car parked in front of the cleaner's, article on pet therapy in the Sunday paper, and so on. By applying image-association to many more contexts, you dramatically improve your recall of all sorts of information. Just think of your mind as a camera, able to record the world in images that you select in more or less detail, according to your needs or interests.

Personal comments (*verbal* elaboration) get you involved both emotionally and intellectually, guaranteeing a vibrant memory trace. Comment on everything you care about, including the image-associations you dream up, and you will remember much more.

Organizing by categories (*associative* elaboration) refers to how information is stored. Both at the time of recording and at the time of recall it pays off to use categories, or general subject headings, which will trigger recall of specific memories. For example, an art object can be categorized in terms of the material it is made of, its size, color, age, place, or value, with subcategories such as decorative, utilitarian, commercial, or sentimental value. If you key the information you are recording to a category, it will be easy to recall the information by invoking that category when thinking of the subject. Instead of being at the mercy of incomplete free recall brought about by chance through involuntary memory, which is often based on a single impression, you can rely on voluntary memory, which is fostered by the use of several categories as cues.

Reviewing and **using** information guarantee the fluency of recall. When you review information you participate actively in the three stages of the memory process: recording, storage, and recall. It is normal to keep in the front of your mind the names of people you deal with frequently, products you use on a daily basis, streets you often go down (provided you have made it a point to notice them!). In my work, I've found I remember far better those examples and quotations that I use regularly. The fluency of recall depends on usage.

If you keep in mind these principles of good retention you will find many applications and your memory will flourish.

30. Is there such a thing as "memory insurance"?

There is no "memory-insurance policy" covering all possible lapses, but following the above principles of good retention combined with using mnemonics is the best package available to prevent forgetting. Prevention is the key to memory performance. Anticipating, becoming more aware, more observant, using strategies to plant cues, is the way to ensure good recall. Driving your memory is comparable to driving a car: partly reflex, partly strategy, essentially a function of practice and experience and good driving habits. It is vulnerable to exterior and interior factors not always easy to control, such as distractions, fatigue, errors of perception or judgment. That is why you should consider yourself lucky to escape most accidents, even if some are inevitable. The better you drive, the safer you feel, and with just reason. Conditioned reflexes facilitating attention prevent many accidents or episodes of forgetfulness. A pause to look around before leaving a place will ensure that you have not forgotten anything, just as it ensures, when the light turns green, that you are not going to be hit by a car running a red light. Good habits and efficient strategies make for safe driving. There is never full protection against the antics of a drunk driver, of course, but by driving defensively you can avoid many situations in which accidents are more likely to occur. Similarly, armed with principles of good retention you can both avoid major memory lapses and accept minor slips without giving them too much importance. Drive your mind safely, and you will not forget so many things.

MEDICAL ISSUES

Memory problems can arise from many causes, some of them medical. In this section, we deal with the pathological conditions—mental and physical, temporary and permanent—that can affect the ability to remember.

1. What is the difference between age-associated memory impairment and Alzheimer's disease?

A very important question, given the media hype about Alzheimer's. This degenerative disease affects the memory mostly of older people, but in its most extreme form, may strike in middle age. Perhaps because the first signs of forgetfulness are the same in everyday life no matter what the source of the problem, the public has been easily confused and unnecessarily worried. The fear is understandable, however: To this day no cure has been found to this insidious form of senile dementia. It is a good idea, therefore, to differentiate between memory deficits related to normal healthy aging and memory deficits related to disease.

Senility, no matter what type, is not part of normal aging. There are qualitative and quantitative differences between the two:

Qualitatively, the memory losses occurring with age are minor, such as temporarily forgetting the names of relations, or a missed appointment. In these cases one is more embarrassed than handicapped. By contrast, in Alzheimer's cases the losses are major: the month or season of the year, or even the spouse's name. As the illness progresses, patients are unable to find their words, and fall into silence, whereas normal elderly people maintain their vocabulary and even manage to increase it, in spite of the frustration they experience when they cannot recall a specific word they want to use: "I have it on the tip of my tongue," they complain. While this happens to everyone at any age, the frequency of such incidents does increase with age. We must accept this fact, and use synonyms in order to maintain communications without creating anxiety. This proves impossible for Alzheimer's patients, whose language-ability processes are rapidly incapacitated. They eventually become aphasic—that is, they have major language difficulty—and cannot communicate the simplest ideas. Thus Alzheimer's patients have not only global memory deficits but other neurological losses as well.

Quantitatively, the differences in memory capacity are even more dramatic. The worst-case scenario for normal subjects shows losses of 30 percent in those over the age of 70. By contrast, in Alzheimer's cases one witnesses losses as high as 90 percent or more, which translates into quasi-total incapacitation, with every piece of memory function virtually destroyed. Normal losses have nothing to do with the other kinds. They are not a prelude to Alzheimer's or any further deterioration. Normal older patients complaining of memory loss have been monitored in many research studies throughout the world, and the results are unanimous: They are no more likely to develop the disease than the average noncomplainer. This becomes understandable when one looks at the causes.

Although in both cases biochemical changes are at work, in the normal aging brain the modest reduction of acetylcholine (a neurotransmitter substance essential to memory function) and the slowing down of cerebral metabolism are associated with psychosocial changes (for instance, disuse of organizational strategies no longer required for work). In the Alzheimer's brain the changes are dramatically different: The neurotransmitters required for memory and attentional function eventually run out. The affected areas are initially localized to the limbic structures and, in particular, the hippocampus, where the reduction of acetylcholine is drastic. In other areas of the brain there are further reductions in the amounts of certain chemicals called biogenic amines, such as noradrenaline, which is essential to focused attention. Moreover, one notices structural changes in Alzheimer's patients not apparent in normal aging: first, a great reduction in the number of nerve cells; and second, the development of abnormal "neurofibrillary tangles" inside nerve cells and deposits of so-called "senile plaque" surrounding them. These lesions are found primarily in certain brain centers of memory and learning: the hippocampus, located in the temporal lobes, and the amygdala, which is part of the limbic system.

One could call these cases "fixation amnesia," because they have suffered damage to the learning and memory processes that fix memories in place. For example, an advanced Alzheimer's patient to whom objects are shown can rarely find the words to name them. He/she is even unable to remember the objects or repeat the words immediately after exposure no matter how great the number of repetitions, which is not the case with normal older people. Thus, at every level of psychology and biochemistry, great differences exist between the two types of memory loss. Furthermore, one is not reversible; the other is, with an appropriate training program.

A piece of advice: Do not watch for signs of mental deterioration you might misinterpret. If you complain about your memory, itemizing all the things you forgot in the past week, chances are you do not suffer from Alzheimer's disease. The unfortunate people who are stricken by it do not usually remember their forgetfulness; they forget that they forgot! It is their family who notices it and points it out to them. Their reaction is predictable, they deny it, whereas you do not. (This statement may be controversial regarding the very early stages of Alzheimer's, in which complaints may appear along with the expected amount of worrying, but it is true of the final diagnosis after the disease progresses.)

Although it is possible to observe the effects of Alzheimer's disease by studying the behavior of the patient, it is only at the time of autopsy that the diagnosis can be confirmed by the structural abnormalities in the brain. To this day we are far from knowing what causes it. Since the disease cannot be predicted from episodes of benign forgetfulness, heredity helps establish the diagnosis in certain cases.

2. Is Alzheimer's disease hereditary?

It is easy to suppose but difficult to prove the hereditary factor. What causes Alzheimer's is still a mystery, as shown in studies of pairs of identical twins; in many cases, only one is stricken. Researchers think that up to 40 percent of cases are hereditary. In certain families it happens that all the children are affected. But in most cases, the risk is not higher than in the rest of the population: 5 to 10 percent of people over 65.

Given the human potential for psychosomatic problems, it is better not to speculate wildly just because you have a parent with the disease. We should do everything possible to fight off anxiety and depression, the main causes of memory troubles in normal people. It is not unusual to see people who have tested "normal" come to my class carrying a magnum dose of anxiety because a parent or spouse suffers from Alzheimer's. The training reassures them because it shows them they can learn and remember. My accent is on action and use of strategies giving immediate results in the memorization of useful information such as names and faces. But I also try to instill a philosophy of the present: Isn't it better to enjoy our mental faculties while we have them instead of fearing their loss?

I am often asked if one can predict the disease. Apart from the hereditary factor, only age seems to matter: Alzheimer's strikes mostly people over the age of 80, of which 20 to 25 percent are thus afflicted. More women than men are victims, simply because more women reach this advanced age. Only 5 percent of all people between 70 and 80 contract Alzheimer's, while of those between 60 and 70 only 3 percent have the disease. Below age 60, the disease is extremely rare and likely to be of hereditary origin, especially when parents were stricken at an early age. In early "presenile" cases the disease progresses rapidly and dramatically—prognosis of five years of life expectancy after diagnosis—whereas in the older patient the prognosis is from five to seven years.

3. Is there a difference between senility and Alzheimer's disease?

The word senility is a contraction of the medical term "senile dementia," which corresponds to a syndrome defined by the loss of mental faculties including memory. This syndrome may result from various causes, one of them being the pathology described by Alois Alzheimer, who first identified the disease.

Other causes of senility different from the Alzheimer's type may be stroke or atherosclerosis.

4. What can one do about a diagnosis of Alzheimer's?

Is Alzheimer's disease treatable? Unfortunately, a cure has not been found yet. One must help the patient live with the affliction for as long as ten years or so, when death from ostensibly other causes occurs. In our aging population, more and more cases are seen (the 80+ group is the fastest growing segment of the population). Fortunately, there is now enough information to help take care of these patients.

First, one must find a doctor specializing in the care of this type of patient. Many physicians in internal medicine, neurology, and psychiatry deal with geriatric cases. They have the necessary experience to help organize the life of the patient. It is important to realize that a feeling of helplessness is at the root of the depression that frequently strikes the patient's family. Half of all caregivers need medical intervention themselves because they become ill as a consequence of stress. It is essential to help them in their tasks so that they can take care of their own needs. Shifts in care must be worked in to allow them to recuperate.

A book entitled *The Thirty-Six Hour Day*, by Nancy Mace and Peter Rabins, answers many practical questions regarding everyday care. Further information can be obtained from the nonprofit Alzheimer's Disease and Related Disorders Association, which has offices in all major cities nationwide.

5. Are there other degenerative diseases affecting memory?

Yes. Like Alzheimer's disease, Pick's and Korsakov's syndromes are also degenerative disorders. The diagnostic differentiation between Alzheimer's and Pick's can only be done postmortem. In general Pick's hits a younger population, between 40 and 60 years of age. It is characterized by rapid deterioration and a neuropathology different from Alzheimer's.

Korsakov's syndrome stems from a lack of vitamins of the B group, and is seen mostly in alcoholics suffering from malnutrition. According to Dr. J.L. Signoret of Paris, who has studied amnesiacs, these patients seem to have more problems with retrieval than with "encoding" (recording). By the time they show symptoms, the lesions are often too pronounced to make repair possible. It is at the level of prevention that one must act: no more three-martini lunches, one-liter-of-wine-per-person meals, no more regular aperitifs and after-dinner drinks! By drinking alcohol in moderation and only occasionally rather than on a regular basis, you can avoid tragic consequences for brain function. There is in fact some evidence that even moderate drinking contributes to increased memory loss in the elderly.

6. Is self-diagnosis of memory problems a good idea?

Yes, if only to decide whether a visit to the doctor or psychologist is warranted. First, determine the gravity of the problem. The Folstein Mini-Mental Examination, a simple test widely used around the world to screen for dementia, contains a key question you can try to answer at home: Choose three common words such as *apple, pen,* and *lake.* Study them as long as you judge it necessary so that you register them. Then set a timer at five minutes, and use this time to do something else, like reading the newspaper, watching TV, or listening to the radio—it is up to you to choose your distraction. *But do not repeat the three words.* When time is up, try to remember them. Alzheimer's patients cannot do so, even in the early stages of the disease. If you miss one or even two words, don't panic! Retake the test a little later. Your results should reassure you right away, because patients with degenerative disease cannot improve their score. They seem to have lost the potential to record information.

If the worst-case scenario materializes and you flunk the test several times in a row, can you conclude that you have the disease? No, because the most common cause of memory troubles associated with age is depression. To determine whether you suffer from depression requiring intervention, answer rapidly and spontaneously the questions of the following Mood Assessment Test. Only, after you take the test will I tell you how to interpret it. *Do not read ahead,* or you risk skewing the results.

Table 1a
Mood Scale

Circle the answer that best describes how you have felt over the past week:

1. Are you basically satisfied with your life?   YES / NO
2. Have you dropped many of your activities and interests?   YES / NO
3. Do you feel that your life is empty?   YES / NO
4. Do you often get bored?   YES / NO
5. Are you in good spirits most of the time?   YES / NO
6. Are you afraid that something bad is going to
     happen to you?   YES / NO
7. Do you feel happy most of the time?   YES / NO
8. Do you often feel helpless?   YES / NO
9. Do you prefer to stay at home, rather than going out
     and doing new things?   YES / NO
10. Do you feel you have more problems with memory
     than most?   YES / NO
11. Do you think it is wonderful to be alive now?   YES / NO
12. Do you feel pretty worthless the way you are now?   YES / NO
13. Do you feel full of energy?   YES / NO
14. Do you feel that your situation is hopeless?   YES / NO
15. Do you think that most people are better off
     than you are?   YES / NO

Answers indicating depression are highlighted in Table 1b. Each answer counts one point; scores greater than 5 indicate probable depression.

7. Is there a cure to depression?

"What can I do if I feel depressed?" "How does one cure depression?" To these questions there is a truly optimistic answer: YES! One can treat depression at any age, even in people over 80. It is mostly due to the loss of chemical substances in the brain called biogenic amines. These substances are not unlike adrenaline, which flows in the blood of young athletes during competitions. Unfortunately, the brain produces less and less of these substances as one grows older. But there are safe medications one can take to replace these natural products, just as one takes vitamins to offset deficiencies. Too many people suffer helplessly when diagnostic methods and treatment are both available. They may not know about them, or they may be afraid of serious side-effects or addiction to drugs. It is true that overuse of benzodiazepines, widely known under the brand names Valium and Halcion, can trigger memory deficits. But a competent psychiatrist knows his/her medications, monitors them, and tailors dosages to the individual's tolerance. Older people are better off going to a geriatric clinic, where the physicians are more familiar with appropriate dosages.

Certain doctors have their pet prescriptions in which they firmly believe. It is up to you to look into it. For instance, Dr. Walter Bortz, a well-known Palo Alto geriatrician, is an adept of exercise as an antidepressant, for it causes the body to manufacture endorphins, which may produce euphoria. Therefore he encourages his patients to follow an exercise program, or at least to walk regularly. Given the risks of strenuous exercise, and the reduced energy of the elderly, his idea may not work for everyone. Indeed, he has his detractors: those who believe in biochemistry and medications. But his fans, who, like him,

Table 1b
Mood Scale
Scoring Key:

Choose the answer that best describes how you have felt over the past week:

1. Are you basically satisfied with your life? YES / **NO**
2. Have you dropped many of your activities and interests? **YES** / NO
3. Do you feel that your life is empty? **YES** / NO
4. Do you often get bored? **YES** / NO
5. Are you in good spirits most of the time? YES / **NO**
6. Are you afraid that something bad is going to happen to you? **YES** / NO
7. Do you feel happy most of the time? YES / **NO**
8. Do you often feel helpless? **YES** / NO
9. Do you prefer to stay at home, rather than going out and doing new things? **YES** / NO
10. Do you feel you have more problems with memory than most? **YES** / NO
11. Do you think it is wonderful to be alive now? YES / **NO**
12. Do you feel pretty worthless the way you are now? **YES** / NO
13. Do you feel full of energy? YES / **NO**
14. Do you feel that your situation is hopeless? **YES** / NO
15. Do you think that most people are better off than you are? **YES** / NO

Danielle C. Lapp

love the outdoors and are more inclined to find "natural cures," are among the healthiest senior citizens.

One notices more cases of depression in northern countries during the long winter period, when the days are extremely short and the sun rarely shines. The effect of light on mood has been documented in Scandinavia, where people with depression are successfully treated by exposure to screens of artificial light placed in front of their desks during working hours. (Pink fluorescent lights are supposed to be particularly pleasant.)

Speaking of color, psychologists have studied the effects of colors on mood and have confirmed what you may already know: Soft pastel and cool colors calm the spirit, while bright ones—in particular the register of "warm" hues like yellow, orange, red—are exciting. Neutrals and dark colors have neither stimulant nor soothing effects but convey seriousness or sadness. Colors' affective connotations vary according to their use: In interior decorating, neutrals may put the accent on sophistication, intimacy, or neutrality. In offices, beige, browns, and grays traditionally dominate: Neither daring nor offensive, they do not call attention to themselves. For clothing and formal attire, dark colors convey authority. They used to be associated with grief, along with mauve and purple, but fashion is changing all that. Taking the influence of color on mood into account, you can choose accordingly how to decorate your place and how to dress when you have the blues.

In offices and homes the colors we live in affect our moods. When my first husband died, I redecorated one room of my home; I am grateful to the decorator friend who helped me choose the right hue of blue. I hesitated between a vivid medium blue with a hint of red and a paler blue with mauve overtones. She said in my state of mind I should go for the vivid one because is it "tonic." The fact is, I have always felt both calm and energized in this room. Since then I have always been more aware of color wherever I go. I have learned that within each

155

color there are hues of other colors, as in the above example. According to your preferences, use color to modify your moods or keep them in check. Although this does not cure depression, it helps chase away the occasional bout of spleen.

Music can also alter mood, if you choose wisely. Although the type of music is a matter of preference, some rhythms and lyrics are uplifting and others are not. Be aware of the effect they have on you. In the classical range, for example, baroque music, with its even-keeled tones and varied movements, is always uplifting, whereas the unpredictable emotional range of some of the romantic and modern pieces oscillate between high and low moods. The baroque composers—Mozart, Haydn, Handel, Bach, Pachelbel—will uplift you. Give them a try whenever you feel sad.

Another suggestion: Group therapy is considered beneficial when the depression has psychosocial causes, as is the case after the death of a relative or some other major loss disrupting everyday life and isolating the person both physically and morally. Sharing feelings and thoughts with people who have gone through a similar situation brings a certain relief, even though it does not eliminate depressive thoughts. At least one realizes one is not suffering alone! In this setting, where sympathetic souls show concern and solidarity, people are more inclined not only to express themselves, but also to listen; whereas when confiding to family or friends, one has the feeling of burdening them with problems they cannot fully understand, not having been there.

Speaking of communication, there are things to say and other things to withhold when talking to a grieving person. Start by avoiding these: "Time heals everything." (Who cares about the future? It is the present that hurts!) "You are too young to remain a widow/widower; you will marry again." (It is not yet time to think about it. He/she wants to remember the dear departed.) "Call me during the week." (He/she feels too vulnerable to call and risk imposing or being rejected; besides, it is during the evenings and on weekends that loneliness is at its worst.) The most important thing is to be available and to listen in a receptive manner.

You can help your friends by allowing them to express their grief, but also by distracting them. Be the one to pick up the phone and call, invite, and organize outings and activities. With time, love, and a return to regular activities, depression should subside; but why not act now, using everything known to influence mood? You will alleviate depression all the more efficiently.

8. Can health problems affect memory?

Yes, and not just depression. All disorders associated with anxiety disturb memory function. Recent studies have shown that certain anxiety disorders, such as agoraphobia (the fear of going out in public) worsen with age to the point of incapacitation. Panic attacks discharge quantities of neuroactive chemicals called catecholamines in the body, causing a psychological effect—despair—as well as a physical one—cardiac symptoms. Diagnosis is possible only through a complete medical examination. The condition, although frequent in the elderly, often escapes hurried physicians.

In fact, doctors themselves may be responsible for one of the most prevalent causes of memory troubles: the overuse of certain medications. The most dangerous, because they are the most often used, are sleeping pills. They make one drowsy or groggy during the day, affecting alertness and attention. Certain cardiac medications exert the same effect. Substances such as propranolol, widely used to control hypertension, can cause depression and memory problems. If you notice changes in your memory performance, look into the medications you are taking. It is good to trust your physician, but there are so many new drugs on the market that he/she may have overlooked some side effects. Among those, the psychological ones are always the last to be taken into consideration.

Many other conditions may bring about memory disturbances if not treated in time: hypertension, diabetes (even minor cases), thyroid disorders, the decline of sight and hearing, and regular exposure to toxins such as pesticides in agriculture and lead in paint, nutritional deficiencies—in particular those associated with alcoholism (See Question #5, this section). Finally come tumors of the brain, which rarely result in memory troubles but more typically give rise to motor troubles and epilepsy.

9. Does sleep influence memory?

If your teachers did not tell you, they should have: Rather than cramming late on the night preceding an exam, get a good night's sleep in order to be able to think clearly with a rested mind when the memory effort is required. This is what the 16th-century French essayist Montaigne meant when he proclaimed: "Better a well-made head than a well-filled one." Indeed, what is the use of remembering information one cannot organize and efficiently employ? Good sense points to regular studying as the only way to assimilate new learning. It is essential to rest the brain, which can be taxed by overwork during the day and by poor sleeping conditions at night. While you sleep, information is revised, manipulated, and stored. It is not rare to wake up with an answer to a question that has been preoccupying you. (If you want to learn how to "incubate a dream" to get specific answers, read psychologist Gayle Delaney's books.)

Bear in mind that sleep is not uniform. Vincent Bloch and his collaborators at France's National Center for Scientific Research maintain that consolidation of memories is the task not of sleep in general, but of the famous "paradoxical sleep" discovered years ago by Eugene Aserinsky and Nathaniel Kleitman in the United States. During this phase of sleep, which lasts for about 20 minutes and occurs every hour and a half in human beings, all the senses are put on hold, disconnecting the brain from the exterior world. It is then that the "maturation of the memory trace" takes place: It is processed, reviewed, consolidated, and finally stored. There is thus a real information-processing operation at work while the brain is "idling." To deprive someone of sleep after learning results in performance inferior to the subject's mental capacity.

However, just as one cannot learn effectively without sleeping, the idea that one could learn while sleeping—a theory called "hypnopedia," illustrated in Aldous Huxley's *Brave New World*—has proven to be just a fairytale. The reason is that both the conscious and the subconscious play a role in memory processes. They are interdependent: One cannot work without the other.

Suggestions: Make sure that you sleep tight the night before a demanding task or a heavy day at work. And get into the habit of reviewing the most important items just before going to bed.

Insomnia has major consequences for mental health. It disturbs not only sleep, but also the waking hours, which are lived in a haze of unreality. Older people in particular, who sleep very little, are deprived of fourth-stage or "deep sleep," during which the system recharges itself, recuperating energy. In a chronic state of fatigue, life is perceived through a dangerous fog. Under these conditions, it is difficult to fix attention and register anything. Richard Coleman, a specialist in chronobiology, underlines the fact that with age, the circadian rhythms lose their flexibility to adjust to changes. Businessmen traveling across time zones are seldom in peak condition to make important decisions. Ideally speaking, they would be better off using their trips only to establish contacts or consolidate deals already made. Lack of sleep affects not only memory but also judgment. Thrown in the effect of alcohol intake during social gatherings, and one is really in bad shape, says Dr. Tom Roth: "People who sleep only five hours a night are handicapped. Those who drink alcoholic beverages are handicapped. And those who sleep only five hours and in addition drink alcohol are superhandicapped."

After years of research in this area, one important finding emerges: Sleep is indispensable to regulate the functions of the human organism. There is no more efficient torture for destroying personality than total sleep deprivation. (See *Amnesty International Reports* for evidence.) It is therefore not astonishing that insomnia (partial deprivation) disrupts the life of those suffering from it. Insomnia strikes mostly the elderly. Although it is normal to sleep a little less as you age, it is not normal to stay awake a good part of the night. The remedy offered by many physicians is sleeping pills, which may cause drowsiness during the day. This in turn leads to a total disruption of life. In my opinion, until effective, safe, drugs whose effects wear off quickly are found, relaxation methods, which have proven effective in some research studies, are preferable.

Still, there is something even worse than insomnia: *Sleep apnea* is a disorder found mostly in men above 60 years of age. It is characterized by numerous sudden arrests in breathing function, which create an oxygen deficit to the brain and the heart. Victims often wake up, startled, with a stifling snore, and often cannot fall back to sleep. They complain of insomnia at night and fatigue during the day. If you are experiencing frequent memory problems and sleep disruptions, don't immediately resort to sleeping pills. You may be suffering from sleep apnea. Check with your doctor. Simple tests can diagnose it, and there are treatments available.

10. Can anesthesia cause memory disturbances?

Yes, if the patient is not sufficiently oxygenated. Even when it is administered under the best conditions, temporary memory disturbances occur during the days following anesthesia, because the medications used during surgery may take several days to be eliminated from the system. Therefore, if you must have surgery, you have everything to gain by communicating to the surgeon and the anesthesiologist your worry about the monitoring of oxygen intake. Warned, they should be more careful in this respect. It is difficult to say how much time must "normally" elapse before fully intact memory returns. This depends on factors too numerous and complex to mention here. Instead of worrying, the only reasonable option is to wait patiently with the assurance that sooner or later your memory will be restored. During this period, avoid stressing yourself with memory challenges and forgive yourself your lapses rather than give them undue importance. Everything will be all right once your body has eliminated the drugs, just give it time.

11. Which chemical substances negatively affect memory?

All medications that cause drowsiness. The list is long, so I will only mention a few: Barbiturates, benzodiazepines and other sedatives, antidepressants, antihistamines, and certain antiepileptic drugs have an immediate effect on memory. Drugs altering perception and consciousness destroy brain cells and precipitate the aging process; LSD, amphetamines, and phencyclidine (PCP) provoke psychoses that can become permanent. Cocaine, heroin, and amphetamines create addictions that sometimes very quickly prove to be fatal. The effects of marijuana are similar to those of alcohol, the harm of which becomes detectable after long-term use.

Alcohol is the most common dependency-producing substance. Christopher Ryan and Nelson Butters have studied the premature decline of mental performance among alcoholics. They noticed that "the scores of alcoholics age 34 to 49 did not differ from those of a control group of normal subjects age 50 to 59; the same proved to be true of alcoholics age 50 to 59 compared to normal subjects age 60 to 65." One thing is certain: Memory and alcohol do not mix well! Alcohol interferes above all with the capacity to learn; it slows down mental functions, which makes for defective recording and storing of information.

College students take heed: Drinking is the enemy of studying!

One notices memory disturbances in alcoholics of all ages. In fact, only a few drinks suffice to cause distortions and omissions in short-term memory. Many studies show that even moderate doses of alcohol affect cognitive processes such as abstraction, information processing, and memory. Alcohol, explain Isabel Birnbaum and Elizabeth Parker, prevents memory traces from solidifying. However, what has been previously recorded in a state of sobriety is not necessarily erased. That is why, paradoxically, in a state of alcohol-induced euphoria one is able to remember things from long ago, but not what was just said or just happened. Moreover, the effects of alcohol take longer to be eliminated than was once thought: At Stanford University, Dr. Jerome Yesavage has studied the effects of alcohol and marijuana on the memory, judgment, and reflexes of airplane pilots. Tests conducted using flight simulators have shown that the acute effects of alcohol last longer than twelve hours, while those of marijuana can linger up to 24 hours.

12. What about caffeine and tobacco?

Researchers working with smokers at UCLA have noted lower performances in short-term memory on verbal tests. At the University of Edinburgh, tests on recall of names and faces have confirmed the finding that memory, both visual and verbal, is impaired in subjects smoking more than one pack a day (a high nicotine intake). Therefore, cigarettes and work are not a good combination, because they interfere with information processing—that is, with the capacity to organize and record.

Why do people smoke? By habit? Out of the need to conform with their peers? One can speculate whether the consumption of cigarettes (as that of alcohol, perhaps) is not in fact linked to anxiety: Many smokers report that they smoke because they are "nervous." By treating one problem, might it be possible to treat the other? Efficient treatments for anxiety reduction and detoxification do exist. Wouldn't it be efficient to set up combined programs?

Caffeine, when used in excessive quantities, provokes agitation, which interferes with memory function. Given the fact that people have their own tolerances, it is possible that a cup of coffee or tea proves beneficial to an elderly person prone to drowsiness. In the ideal state for memory performance, the mind is both alert and relaxed. When chemical substances become addictive, they prevent us from achieving relaxation. Better then, to reach for alternative solutions to appease the nerves: herb tea, decaf, chewing gum—or even an object to handle, like a "pet rock" or the rosary beads the Greeks fondle all day long.

13. Do memory troubles subside once these substances are discontinued?

It depends on the age and the degree of deterioration. Among older people rebounds do not always occur, because a lifetime of abuse has caused irreversible damage. However, certain research studies give grounds for optimism. According to Elizabeth Loftus, most alcohol-induced memory troubles seem to disappear when the person stops drinking: "The performances of alcoholics tested after four or five weeks of treatment were much better," she observes. Not everyone has the same susceptibility to alcohol. Whether you feel the effects of alcohol after one or after several glasses makes a difference in how much of the toxic substance you can ultimately take in. In addition, women are in general more susceptible to the toxic effects of alcohol than men, especially as regards short-term memory function. Among alcoholics, women also seem to suffer from both verbal and spatial cognitive problems, whereas men seem to be only affected by spatial cognitive troubles only, declare alcoholism researchers Marilyn Jones and Ben Morgan Jones. How should we interpret these results? Could it be simply that women talk more and therefore notice this verbal slippage more readily?

My personal observation is that all talkative people—male or female—of a certain age are more likely to complain of the tip-of-the-tongue phenomenon, for the simple reason that they attempt to use more words.

Bottom line: The sooner one stops using alcohol or other substances, the better the chances of recovering the use of one's memory.

14. What is the relationship between hypnosis, psychoanalysis, truth serum, and memory?

Hypnosis, psychoanalysis, and truth serum all aim at dissolving anxiety, the block that prevents memories from resurfacing at the level of consciousness. Hypnosis achieves its goal through the use of suggestion, in a calming environment, by a reassuring therapist who encourages the person to express the anxiety-producing thoughts that are blocking recall. Hypnosis and auto-hypnosis (or self-suggestion) produce a relaxed state of mind in which associations can liberate memories.

Psychoanalysis deals with bigger blocks, at work since infancy. It aims at revealing the self-protecting mechanisms the mind has created to suppress traumatic memories. The question of these memories' authenticity remains controversial: It is not clear whether the emerging memory is accurate, or just fabricated to please the therapist. It is legitimate to question all methods of questioning that suggest the answers the questioner hopes to elicit. A subject can indeed be manipulated under questioning—court lawyers and judges can testify to this. That is why testimonies obtained under hypnosis are generally not accepted in court.

The modern pharmacological equivalent to these psychological interventions is "truth serum" or sodium amytal, a short-term-acting barbiturate that is infrequently used in psychiatric diagnosis when a patient is too anxious to talk about key symptoms. In this context, the drug is effective.

15. Is a memory pill available today?

No. As we have mentioned earlier, there is no known cure to degenerative diseases such as Alzheimer's. The chemistry of the brain being extremely complex, the causes of the depletion of its neurotransmitter chemicals, substances that are not easily replaced, have not yet been discovered.

By contrast, it is possible to help people with age-associated memory impairment. The biological and psychological changes related to aging are well known, and most are reversible. For instance, on the biological level, depression is linked to depletions of catecholamines in the brain; your doctor can prescribe a treatment to restore them. However, it is much more difficult to replace acetylcholine in the brain, because it plays an important role throughout the entire body. Any manipulation of this substance has multiple uncontrollable repercussions.

In spite of these difficulties, pharmaceutical research continues. There are already a few products available in Europe, such as Hydergine, manufactured by Sandoz in Switzerland and used for many years for memory enhancement without major problems. This drug seems to reactivate brain metabolism as well as to increase the supply of the catecholamines. Another drug made in France by Ipsen, Tanakan, also has an effect on nerve-cell metabolism. Phosphatidylserine, a natural substance purified in Italy by Fidia, is particularly promising because it replaces a chemical that decreases in quantity with age but is essential to the structure of nerve cells. *These drugs do not work miracles, but many people have reported beneficial effects while using them.* Ask your doctor about them. He/she can tell you if they are appropriate in your case.

Finally, as has been demonstrated for more than thirteen years of our controlled studies at Stanford University, the psychological methods I have been showing you can improve memory at any age. Before resorting to drugs, try these mental strategies. There is no risk of any negative side effect using them, but a very good chance of the positive satisfaction of understanding what you are doing that produces recall. The feeling of control is worth a million dollars, because it restores not only memory but also self-confidence.

REFLECTIONS ON MEMORY

There is more to memory, of course, than science. Memory is the foundation on which the edifice of one's identity is constructed. This section raises questions that may linger in our minds.

1. Do memories play a major role in my life?

Do you live in the present, or do you tend to rehash the past? Is reminiscing part of your daily activity? Are you interested in history, the past, antiques? Do you wish you had lived in another era? Do you enjoy feeling nostalgic? Would you lyrically say to your beloved, as did the French poet Paul-Jean Thoulet: "My memory embraces you throughout the past . . ."? Do you have difficulty getting rid of old things? Are you a pack rat, filling your closets with clothing and objects?

If you have answered yes to these questions, chances are you are inclined towards the past, and memories play a major part in your life. In your constant comparisons of past and present, you value the past more, perhaps because it is gone and irretrievable. You are thus drawn to relive scenes from the past by looking at objects surrounding you, especially pictures and souvenirs associated with a person, a place, or an event. You get attached to objects that remind you of memories you want to cultivate. The events of the present continuously send you flashbacks.

Perhaps you see your life in continuity: "I am the result of my lived past. By reviewing each significant episode, each important person, I gain a perspective of what shaped me as I am now." This outlook allows you to assert your roots. It is very different from the outlook of those who, anchored in the present, want to forget by turning the page on the past. For them, one thing— a slice of life, a person, a home—replaces another. This ideal universe of the eternal present is autonomous and self-sufficient; it need not be explained or justified by the past. But it does not really exist, for it is impossible to cut oneself off completely from one's past. Several movies have treated this theme: *The Silence* by Ingmar Bergman and Bertolucci's *Last Tango in Paris* both show two main characters trying to establish an intimate rapport without saying anything about their past. In *The Silence*, the female protagonist specifically seeks the reduced communication inherent between strangers unable to speak a common language, under the pretext of wanting to concentrate exclusively on the language of the senses. Likewise, in *Last Tango*, the mature Marlon Brando exerts his authority to orchestrate his sexual prowess with a very young woman in an empty apartment devoid of any references, by forbidding her to ask any personal question or talk about herself. In both cases, although the dialogue is reduced to the minimum, the characters cannot help making references to their past, or wondering about the other one's past, which they perceive as a failure. Ultimately, it could be said that one does not exist in the instant, even at the level of the pure sensation, because one cannot escape thinking. Any thought triggers associations and past references.

From my personal observation, I would venture to say that more women tend to see their lives as a continuity of attachments whereas more men see theirs as a series of independent episodes. If this proved to be true, could it explain the often-encountered feminine predilection for relationships and masculine predilection for action? If one wants to act, one must focus on the present and put aside the past, at least temporarily. But there are some who act like the ant from Aesop's fable, with the future in mind; whereas others act like the cicada, with only the will to live and enjoy the present without worrying about what tomorrow will bring. It is easy to guess who, of the two, takes time to pause and remember.

Depending on the role memories play in our lives, we give them more or less importance. Each episode of recall reinforces them, but also modifies them; our recollections are prompted by specific contexts or moods, which vary constantly. When we spend our time reminiscing, we are less available in the present, which limits our attention.

2. What are the pros and cons of living in the past?

Whoever lives in the past, surrounded by memories, has a gap to fill in the present. By escaping into the past (or the future), the person takes refuge against the often-disappointing daily reality. This attitude can be temporarily beneficial, as is the case when a loved one dies or when you have been uprooted. As the present appears impersonal, empty, neutral, even hostile, it is necessary to fill it with comforting images and emotions drawn from the recent past.

During a period of grief or adaptation, the focus shifts back into the past. Paradoxically, it is the roots—the memory of the loved one or the country of origin—that feed the emotional elements needed for reconstruction of a new present independent from this past. Therefore, it is wise to accept this nostalgic condition while engaging in the daily actions that will build one's new life. Day by day, one develops new habits, new activities, new goals, new acquaintances, and one learns to live without the person or place one has lost. Memories bridge this gap of solitude. It is actually beneficial to activate memories of the departed, rather than suppress them.

However, to indulge in living in the past (often idealized because only the rosy part is remembered) risks cutting yourself off from reality. Edgar Allan Poe's *The Raven* illustrates the obsessional, desperate thoughts converging on the death of a loved one: "Nevermore, nevermore. . . ." croaks the raven. By rehashing over and over the theme of the impossibility of a loved one's return to life, you can easily fall prey to despair. The only way to heal is by focusing on the present. Nature, friends, books, work, and responsibilities are more than diversions: They are the tools of reconstruction. When I arrived in California, I missed certain aspects of French culture—to name a few, the cafes and Paris! My husband helped me adjust by lovingly pointing out that as long as I concentrated on what I missed, I couldn't enjoy what I had here and did not have there. So, day after day, I proceeded to demystify those sorely missed cafes— where, come to think of it, I used to spend very little time—and Paris, whose attractions I, like most working Parisians, seldom took advantage of. I started focusing on my beautiful house; my garden, a true oasis of quiet and nature; the beauty and the cosmopolitan flavor of the San Francisco Bay area—the parks, the Pacific Ocean, the woods so close to civilization, Stanford's easy yet stimulating life, the energy of the region, the proximity of the Sierra Nevada mountain range. In order to adjust, you must have at least one foot grounded in the present.

Complementing the will to embrace the present are strategies for doing so. Observation training facilitates concentration, as we have seen in preceding sections; it also helps immerse oneself momentarily in a subject. It is during my grief period that I discovered the joys of gardening. I observed, for example, that when cutting flowers, I could stimulate the growth by cutting them at certain parts of the stem, thereby sparing tiny buds unnoticed until then. Stimulating new interests puts you on the way to rebuilding a present. When the past plays second fiddle, it loses its dominance. No longer does it overwhelm the present in our minds. Then memories can be liberated to enrich the present without risk of our being overwhelmed by them. As Kierkegaard wrote: "To understand life one must look backward, but to live it one must move forward."

3. How can I rid myself of painful memories?

Simply by avoiding bringing them back to the surface. This does not prove easy to do when one is the victim of obsessional thoughts linked to a painful past. To deal with this kind of psychological problem, one must see a specialist. But in most cases, you can choose to be around people who will be tactful enough not to bring up subjects that hurt your feelings. And if they do, through ignorance or carelessness, it is up to you to change the subject without further ado. You can also prevent the return of painful memories by avoiding places associated with personal disasters. Sometimes this entails going out of one's way, as I did for years in order to avoid the hospital where I saw my first husband disappear.

We seldom realize how much the surroundings we live in are filled with visual cues recalling people or situations from the past. Getting rid of objects can rid us of the constant irritation of involuntary memory. It took me years to realize the source of the malaise I felt at regular intervals every time I came across objects with which I had negative associations: a poorly repaired silver spoon, a purse so heavy that it gave me a backache every time I used it, a lovely pair of shoes so uncomfortable they gave me blisters every time I walked in them, clothes in which I did not feel at ease or which reminded me of difficult times. Once you have identified the source of painful associations, *get rid of the object*. This may not seem easy to those who, attached to the status quo, are reluctant to change their surroundings. As for the pack rats, they accumulate things without ever discarding any, overloading their closet shelves as well as their memory. One neat way to clean up is giving to charity: You help others at the same time that you help yourself.

A somewhat more serious personal example: After my husband died, I made the mistake, for several years, of leaving his desk as he had used it the last day of his life. Laziness? No, I actually rearranged books on the shelves. Sentimentalism? Who knows? I think people may not want to remove traces of the loved one, for they see it as abandoning, even betraying him or her. The result in my case was that in spite of the new shelf arrangement and the new name given to his study (now "the library"), this place remained a mausoleum until I finally put away the books and documents on his desk. Shortly afterward I felt like moving one painting around and adding another new one. I also bought a Persian carpet, and after the huge 1989 earthquake, I placed the cat's bed under the desk. Could it be the cat who made the difference? All of a sudden the room came alive! Reading the story, *Murr the Cat*, by E.T.A. Hoffman, I started fantasizing that my cat Oceli, like Murr, makes the most of his stays in his master's library to get an education. This room is now the source of multiple pleasant associations, both old and new.

For some people, objects recover their intrinsic value rapidly after the loss of a loved one: "A pen is a pen, this is a good pen, and I am going to use it." Know yourself and act accordingly.

Of course, time allegedly heals all wounds, and someday you may be happy to wear your father's watch without tears welling up in your eyes. Therefore, put aside valuable objects that have sentimental value but that you cannot handle emotionally yet. You may rediscover them later with joy, and without pain.

4. How can we best use the past to make ourselves miserable?

It helps to have masochistic inclinations, but as the leading advocate of the therapy of paradox, Paul Watzlawick, points out in his book *The Situation is Hopeless, but Not Serious: The Pursuit of Unhappiness*, anyone can use the past to make himself miserable. All that is necessary is to play "The Four Games with The Past":

1) Indulge in the glorification of the past, seen "through a rosy filter that screens out everything but the good and beautiful."

2) Follow "our biblical preceptress, Mrs. Lot." Despite the Lord's warning not to look back when fleeing Sodom, she could not resist the temptation, and was changed into a pillar of salt.

3) Hold onto the firm belief that the past cannot be erased, and cling to it, licking the wound of eternal remorse that goes back to the original sin. Keep repeating: "I should have known better, but now it is too late." Persuade yourself that the cause of man's unhappiness depends on forces beyond him: God, heredity, a past error, early childhood, his mother, Eve.

4) Keep on doing "more of the same"; that is, continue doing what you have always done, without asking yourself if there are other solutions. Above all, never question the idea that "there is only ONE solution."

To Watzlawick's advice I would add this one piece: Avoid *humor* at all costs. It could cast a new perspective on things.

By clinging to a distorted past, you will succeed in failing, and thereby guarantee your maximum unhappiness.

5. What is the point of cultivating memories?

I propose three good reasons: To give a sense of continuity and a perspective to your life, to relive privileged moments with the force of the imagination, and to enhance the present.

The pleasure of forgetting momentarily lies in rediscovering people, places, and things. Each season when I review my wardrobe, I delight in rediscovering garments I had put out of my mind for nearly a year. If asked to describe the content of my closet, I would at any given time probably omit half of it. On seeing them again, the recognition is instantaneous, and multiple memories spring back: where I bought them, where I wore them, with whom, the role they played on a trip. If I give myself more time to reminisce, I can recapture a host of memories from simple clothes which act as catalysts of emotions. Past and present merge and unite in objects. People disappear, but their personal objects remain. Thanks to those objects, one can relive special moments of the past—which can be sources of either joy or sorrow. Baudelaire said that "All the echoes of memory, if they could be awakened simultaneously, would form a concert, pleasant or painful, but logical and without dissonances," because it would reflect the complexity of the individual and his experience. But neither logic nor lack of dissonance necessarily equates with happiness or well-being. Unless you are a masochist at heart or suffering from melancholia, you undoubtedly often feel the need to root out a bad memory. As the French poet Aragon writes:

> I tore up my life and my poem . . .
> I tore up my book and my memory
> There were too many black hours within

Easier said than done! To forget bad memories, it helps to cultivate the good ones. By often summoning happy memories you will reinforce them, and prevent the bad ones from showing up. For example, when the first recall association with a person or a place is negative, do not dwell on it, but instead, immediately substitute a positive one. Why allow an unpleasant innkeeper to overshadow all the good experiences of your vacation? By focusing on the latter you will soon leave the unpleasant memories to slumber in your subconscious.

As long as we remember the dead, they are alive within us. The monument to soldiers killed in the Vietnam War, erected in Washington, D.C., is particularly moving in its simplicity: a wall of shiny black granite on which are engraved the names of all who died. (Aren't soldiers' names usually the first to disappear into anonymity?) The surest way to keep memories alive is to recall them at any opportunity, resorting to rituals, objects, and thoughts. Without minimizing the value of public and private commemorations, isn't it better to think often about a loved one than simply to go once a year to the cemetery?

We cultivate memories by the private choices we make. If we surround ourselves with objects charged with associations, and if we linger on them, we trigger voluntarily a chain of memories linked to the mood of those past moments. According to our temperament, we perceive life as a concert in a minor or a major mode. This is clear in the works of many artists—for example, filmmakers Ingmar Berman, Woody Allen, Steven Spielberg, and Mel Brooks, each of whom works with his distinct emotional palette to paint the world in a different hue. We express our outlooks in many ways, including the choices we make to cultivate certain memories at the expense of others.

6. What role does reminiscing play in life?

Reminiscing seems to be part of everyday communication. At any age, people like to talk about their past for two main reasons: first, the pleasure of talking about themselves, and second, to attract our sympathy by allowing us to know and understand them better. Friends and family members reminisce together to express themselves and redefine their bond. Sharing experiences seems essential to emotional balance. Those who typically with-draw from sharing often may suffer from emotional problems going back to their infancy and a solitary childhood.

The human need for reminiscing varies according to the individual and the season of his/her life. Even children, no matter what their age, talk about their past experiences. When one is young, one talks about one's childhood in the hope of building intimate relationships recognizing mutual affinities. In middle life, one feels the need to make an assessment of what has been accomplished up to now, to turn inwards for a moment to find out which direction one has taken, whether it is time to change, and what one wishes to accomplish during the second part of life. It proves easier to explain today's feelings in relation to what one has gone through. By expressing them, one makes it easier for others to understand.

Old-age reminiscences are often coated with sadness—and sometimes bitterness, if people feel they have wasted away their life. At this age, when time becomes scarcer every day, the balance sheet of deeds cannot be rectified, losses must be count-ed. But in general, people like to recall the good times, unless they are depressed. Reminiscing is an opportunity to show the young how they lived their youth, in a way that lionizes them.

Last-minute reminiscences before dying are necessary to a last reconciliation with the world, with oneself, and with God if one is a believer. They foster a spiritual reflection that allows one to accept one's life, and even one's death.

It is generally pleasant and enriching to speak about the past, no matter what your stage in life, but in particular at the end. That proves evident when listening to old people. They tend to tell stories in part to show they too were once our age and lived life fully. They often repeat the same older stories—not because they are senile, but because they want to express something others refuse to hear.

Research on the subject suggests that elderly people who

indulge in constructive reminiscing are emotionally healthier. Dr. Robert Butler, founder of the National Council on Aging, developed the theory of the "life review," which calls for *actively listening to older persons, asking them about the emotions underlying their stories* in order to understand what they mean to them. The interest shown by the listener shows immediate results; it improves the quality of communication. For instance, ask this kind of question: "What did you feel at the time?" Or identify the emotion: "Weren't you excited (or angry)?" Or empathize: "How embarrassing (or painful) that must have been!" This way of listening places the story in its emotional context, which allows the teller to elaborate on it. It seems that, once expressed and acknowledged by others, these emotions need to be expressed less often, which reduces the frequency of recall of this particular story.

It is possible to establish a questionnaire allowing the older person to express the feelings behind the stories they tell. Several models exist for organizing a program of life review.[1]

The success of such programs varies with the individual recipient, but in general people are happy about being given attention, for old age is often perceived as devaluating in no small part because of the lack of interest from society and the young.

In any case, old age recedes in the mind as long as health and optimism can be maintained. An 88-year-old lady I know once expressed her astonishment at catching a glimpse of herself in a mirror: "Margaret! Is that you? I do not feel THAT old!" As Mae West put it, a woman is as old as her feelings, and a man

---

[1] I found Barbara Haight's model, as used by the American Association of Retired Persons, particularly interesting because it is well structured into several sessions covering: the attitude of the person towards reminiscing, childhood, adolescence, family and home, adult age and work, retirement and old age, and the synthesis, resolution, integration and separation from the "new" friend, the interviewer.

is old when he has none. Because old age is the only time of life without a future, it is essential to live the present to the utmost. And since you cannot escape dreaming, you necessarily replace fantasies of the future with evocations of the past. Reminiscing assumes its true value as life draws to its end, because in order to remember, one must have lived.

7. Does one choose to forget?

Generally speaking we forget because we are too absorbed in the present to take the time to evoke the past. When one chooses to forget, one eliminates negative memories first, to protect oneself from being hurt again and again—a human reflex that makes life easier. This is true of the community as well as the individual. Just think of the public reaction in France to the trial of Klaus Barbie, the Nazi criminal called "The Butcher of Lyons" or, in the U.S., the government's belated apology for the internment of Japanese Americans during World War II, both of which bring back unpleasant memories from a bygone era. The moral issue is: "What justifies stirring up the past? Can one correct mistakes by bringing to justice criminals who have up to now escaped indictment?" No matter what the answer to this question might be, some think that truth must come out at all costs. In Germany, this theme was brought to the screen by Michael Verhoeven, in his movie called *"Das Schreckliche Madchen* ("that terrible girl"): Having won a literary prize offered by the city, a young girl embarks upon a search for information on what local personalities did during the Nazi era. She encounters fierce resistance, which instead of deterring her stimulates her to dig even further. This quest for knowledge of what actually happened becomes an obsession, and she ends up alienating everyone, including her family, which had supported her against the virulent attacks of the community. As she becomes famous throughout the whole country, however, local authorities suddenly change their attitude, eventually hiring an artist to sculpt her face. In the last scene, the masterpiece is unveiled during a ceremony honoring her for her civic action. Her stunning reaction is to refuse this honor because it is meant to terminate further inquests—to "turn her into stone" by buying her silence. But she will not be bought out. This film forces us to think hard: Should one choose to forget past political actions, or should one keep remembering them? What are the consequences in both cases? How long should one go on inquiring?

One could find many examples demonstrating that one deliberately chooses to forget; and inversely, that one keeps memories alive by voluntarily recalling them to consciousness. It is interesting to notice how selective forgetting usually is. Most Americans have chosen to remember only the heroic exploits of Charles Lindbergh, showing over and over the news clips of Lindbergh as a triumphant aviator or as a father torn by the kidnapping of his child. His pro-Nazi activity has been erased by the mere fact of not recalling it to the public's awareness. Rare documentaries of events leading up to World War II mention the other side of the hero's life in the "America First" movement. Then there is Louise Rinser, a prolific German writer who at the age of 80 "refused" to remember her writings under the Third Reich, probably because of her present political involvement with the Green Party. There is a continuum of moral judgments regarding such selective forgetfulness: Depending on one's opinions, one opts for truth at any cost or for "leaving well enough alone," taking refuge in the comfort of forgetting.

Beyond these two extreme attitudes there is a third, more objective, wholistic perspective. As shadows, by highlighting a subject bathed in light, enhance the realism of a painting, likewise human foibles and memory lapses reveal the whole experience, a mix of positive and negative, light and dark. The works of Louise Rinser and Lindbergh's life reflect the tensions of the 20th century. According to what one chooses to review, one will remember different factors that made these two individuals famous.

There is no doubt that the media and our cultural heritage influence our choices. The point is to understand why each one of us chooses to forget: simply because it is practical and sometimes necessary to survive. While it proves impossible for people having gone through the Holocaust or the War to erase certain scenes from their mind, most of them have managed to put them aside in order to live happily in the present. From this point of view, forgetting is normal and desirable for the individual. Those who are haunted by horrible images of the inhumanity of man to man need professional help.

But for the community, the knowledge of history is essential in order to avoid the errors of the past. Society must constantly recall the dangers and tragic consequences of racism, anti-Semitism, anti-ommunism, and the medieval witch hunts—all of the ways man seeks and finds scapegoats when he feels threatened. Just as one may choose to forget, one may choose to remember for the well-being of the individual or the community. In this case one must allow oneself to review unpleasant scenes in the hope that they will act as a deterrent to history's repeating itself. And too bad if, in the process, heroes are knocked down from their pedestals!

8. Doesn't forgetting prove convenient? Perhaps too convenient?

Forgetting has positive or negative consequences, depending on the context. It is indispensable to momentarily forget many things in order to concentrate your attention on a task, and to live in the present after traumatic events. Alas, it is also "practical" to forget errands you do not want to run, delicate messages to transmit, appointments you dread. In these cases you can subconsciously forget, just to get off the hook. Famous examples come easily to mind, such as former President Ronald

Reagan failing to remember the circumstances of the sale of arms to Iran. Because of his age, he may be given the benefit of the doubt. But many people choose to forget (or pretend to forget) what can be used against them. In private as well as in public life, it happens all the time. In the French magazine *Le Point*, Jean François Revel has written: "During election time, society replaces memory events with memory lapses. It is not surprising that candidates would rewrite history, especially incumbents eager to expurgate or embellish their contributions. But that the public, in its majority, would forget recent obvious events that could easily mock certain candidates' pretensions, is more mysterious." Revel goes on to blame the evening news, with its rapid succession of brief subjects all presented on the same level, an important piece of information next to a trivial one. Given the fast pace of the presentation, a news item replaces the previous one on the screen and in memory. The memory traces that leave a mark are those that are coated with emotion, which is why political campaign advertisements in the U.S. concentrate on attacking the opponent, and show their favored candidate surrounded by children and flags—simple but moving patriotic symbols. The electable candidate must utter reassuring words that everyone wants to hear, such as George Bush's "Read my lips: NO more taxes!" These stratagems are not new, but are the tools of all propaganda, be it from the left or the right. To win, one must manipulate the memory of the people, which is done with strong slogans and pictures repeated at regular intervals. Forgetting can indeed be a tool of attack or defense, a weapon against others.

To the question of the French writer Robert Desnos: "Can I defend my memory against forgetting?", one must say, yes! But it is not simple. We must constantly be on the lookout, aware of memory's mechanisms and of how easy it is to manipulate memory.

9. Why are we so afraid of forgetting?

To understand why we are so afraid of forgetting, we must ponder what happens when we forget: The event or the people cease to exert an influence on us. It is as if they had never existed. This negation of existence is anxiety-producing. It deprives us in a way of part of our identity, since we too are bound to disappear. Moreover, it is frightening to realize that the death of a loved one is accompanied by the death of all the memories he or she alone could bring back. We are afraid of forgetting because we are afraid of losing ourselves, by losing a piece of our past. This is what minorities living in a foreign country want to avoid at all costs. Therefore they cultivate their language, rites, and cultural identity, clustering in enclaves within the community. Because they fear assimilation, they forbid themselves and their children to forget their origins.

To fight against forgetting takes an organized effort. Some authors have devoted their lives to remembering events too easily forgotten in a world where one war is succeeded by another, or one tyranny replaces another, as do, episodically, natural disasters. I will mention only one example, that of Milan Kundera, whose novels assert his will to remember the historic past of his country, Czechoslovakia. Although most of his characters, like himself, live in exile, they cannot forget their origins. In the novel entitled *The book of Laughing and Forgetting*, Kundera addresses the issue of why we are so afraid of forgetting by raising the question of the role forgetting plays in the lives of individuals and institutions. For Tamina, like her country, forgetting means the end of existence: "If the trembling building of memories crumbles like a poorly anchored tent, there will be nothing left of Tamina but the present, this invisible point, this nothingness slowly advancing towards death." This depressing perspective mirrors that of the exiled author, who always tries to keep in focus the history of his country, pillaged as it was by the Communist regime of Gustav Husak. He reminds us of it in all his novels, because, as he puts it: "To forget is to die." This he learned from those who tried to obliterate the democratic past of his country: "To liquidate the people, Hubl said, one begins by removing their memory." Therefore, one gets rid of the opposition or old former collaborators, who disappear not only in the flesh but on official photographs. This rape of history is unbearable to Kundera, and he applies himself to restoring the balance by forcing people to remember. His books transport us to the universe of a sad and dismantled Prague, to which he cannot go back without suffering from his awareness that his people have resigned themselves to forgetting.

In the last part of the novel I have quoted, Tamina tries to recover from her husband's death. But as soon as she seems to be forgetting him, she feels guilty, as if he had died a second time within her. Then, in a fantasy, an adolescent angel named Rafael transports her to a realm "where things are as light as a breeze, where things are weightless, where remorse does not exist." But Tamina soon finds this world of forgetfulness to be immoral and, finally, unbearable. Kundera is clearly taking sides against forgetting, which, while it may ease the pain, does so at the risk of a greater evil: "To forget is to die."

10. Are memory and creativity related?

The new is rarely original in all its parts. Memory plays a key role in artistic creation. From the manner in which an artist gets his inspiration to the technical means he uses to realize it, he uses memory—no matter what he thinks. There are different ways of doing this, of course. The writer Stendhal said: "I do not make an outline. For me, memory's work extinguishes the glow of imagination." Rather than try to memorize notes elaborated *a priori*, Stendhal preferred to track spontaneous associations. As appetite comes while eating, ideas come while thinking or setting words down on paper; they simply flood one's consciousness without any specific memory effort involved.

However, the creative mind does not create in the void, but from what it has seen, heard, lived, felt, thought before—from *memory*, that is.

As to the contents of creative works, it is obvious that *remembering* often plays a role in the structure of novels, and detective stories in particular. Movies frequently employ the flashback technique, whereby events preceding the first scenes are shown later. The to-and-fro movement between past and present constitutes the dynamic of many a narrative. Sometimes, as is the case with Proust or Kundera, it becomes the main theme.

No matter what the art form—literature, painting, sculpture, architecture, or design—inspiration has its source in memory. The artist transposes the remembered reality, grafting new elements borrowed from his or her imagination. Indeed, whenever we think, we cannot help calling on references to the past. Memory's work is itself a creative process. We select, choose to forget or cultivate memories, and we experience the surprises of involuntary memory. Isn't this combination of the predictable and the unpredictable more than enough to make life interesting?

ABOUT THE AUTHOR

Danielle C. Lapp was born in Toulon, on the French Riviera, in 1944. After visiting the United States on a Fulbright scholarship in 1964 and receiving advanced degrees in English and French from the universities of Paris–Sorbonne, Strasbourg, and Nice, she moved to the United States in 1969 with her first husband, Professor John Lapp of Stanford University's Department of French. Widowed in 1977, she was recruited the following year by Dr. Jerome Yesavage, of Stanford Medical School's Department of Psychiatry, to develop and teach a memory-training course for older adults, as part of his research on age-associated memory impairment.

On Lapp's recommendation, a pre-training segment, focusing on observation and relaxation techniques, was added to the standard mnemonic training that had proven successful in younger people. Thus modified, the memory-training course immediately began to demonstrate strong results; Lapp has been teaching it continuously ever since, still in conjunction with the Yesavage lab, to groups varying in size from 10 to 40. Her former students now number well into the thousands.

Lapp's other books on memory include *Don't Forget! Easy Exercises for a Better Memory at Any Age* (McGraw-Hill, 1987) and *Increasing Your Memory Power* (Barron's, 1992). She enjoys movies, literature, travel, conversation (in five languages), music, and outdoor sports.

The Portable Stanford Book Series

This is a volume of the Portable Stanford Book Series, published by the Stanford Alumni Association. Subscribers receive each new Portable Stanford volume on approval. The following books may also be ordered, by number, on the adjoining card:

$12.95 titles
- *(Nearly) Total Recall: A Guide to a Better Memory at Any Age* by Danielle C. Lapp (#4061)
- *The Disappearing Border: U.S.-Mexico Relations to the 1990s* by Clint E. Smith (#4058)
- *Race Relations on Campus: Stanford Students Speak* by John H. Bunzel (#4062)
- *The Sleepwatchers* by William C. Dement (#4059)
- *Around California in 1891* by Terence Emmons (#4060)
- *Technology and Culture: A Historical Romance* by Barry M. Katz (#4057)
- *2020 Visions: Long View of a Changing World* by Richard Carlson and Bruce Goldman (#4055)
- *"What Is to Be Done?" Soviets at the Edge* by John G. Gurley (#4056)
- *Brief Lessons in High Technology: A Primer on Seven Fields that Are Changing Our Lives* edited by James Meindl (#4045)
- *Terra Non Firma: Understanding and Preparing for Earthquakes* by James M. Gere and Haresh C. Shah (#4030)

$10.95 titles
- *Notable or Notorious? A Gallery of Parisians* by Gordon Wright (#4052)
- *This Boy's Life* by Tobias Wolff (#4050)
- *Ride the Tiger to the Mountain: T'ai Chi for Health* by Martin and Emily Lee and JoAn Johnstone (#4047)
- *Alpha and Omega: Ethics at the Frontiers of Life and Death* by Ernlé W.D. Young (#4046)
- *Conceptual Blockbusting* (third edition) by James L. Adams (#4007)
- *In My Father's House: Tales of an Unconformable Man* by Nancy Huddleston Packer (#4040)
- *The Imperfect Art: Reflections on Jazz and Modern Culture* by Ted Gioia (#4048)
- *Yangtze: Nature, History, and the River* by Lyman P. Van Slyke (#4043)
- *The Eagle and the Rising Sun: America and Japan in the Twentieth Century* by John K. Emmerson and Harrison M. Holland (#4044)
- *The American Way of Life Need Not Be Hazardous to Your Health* (revised edition) by John W. Farquhar, M.D. (#4018)

- *Cory Aquino and the People of the Philippines* by Claude A. Buss (#4041)
- *Under the Gun: Nuclear Weapons and the Superpowers* by Coit D. Blacker (#4039)
- *50: Midlife in Perspective* by Herant Katchadourian, M.D. (#4038)
- *Wide Awake at 3:00 A.M.: By Choice or By Chance?* by Richard M. Coleman (#4036)
- *Hormones: The Messengers of Life* by Lawrence Crapo, M.D. (#4035)
- *Panic: Facing Fears, Phobias, and Anxiety* by Stewart Agras, M.D. (#4034)
- *Who Controls Our Schools? American Values in Conflict* by Michael W. Kirst (#4033)
- *Matters of Life and Death: Risks vs. Benefits of Medical Care* by Eugene D. Robin, M.D. (#4032)
- *On Nineteen Eighty-Four* edited by Peter Stansky (#4031)
- *The Musical Experience: Sound, Movement, and Arrival* by Leonard G. Ratner (#4029)
- *Challenges to Communism* by John G. Gurley (#4028)
- *Cosmic Horizons: Understanding the Universe* by Robert V. Wagoner and Donald W. Goldsmith (#4027)
- *Beyond the Turning Point: The U.S. Economy in the 1980s* by Ezra Solomon (#4026)
- *The Age of Television* by Martin Esslin (#4025)
- *Insiders and Outliers: A Procession of Frenchmen* by Gordon Wright (#4024)
- *Mirror and Mirage: Fiction by Nineteen* by Albert J. Guerard (#4023)
- *The Touch of Time: Myth, Memory, and the Self* by Albert J. Guerard (#4022)
- *The Politics of Contraception* by Carl Djerassi (#4020)
- *Economic Policy Beyond the Headlines* by George P. Shultz and Kenneth W. Dam (#4017)
- *Law Without Lawyers: A Comparative View of Law in China and the United States* by Victor H. Li (#4015)
- *The World That Could Be* by Robert C. North (#4014)
- *America: The View from Europe* by J. Martin Evans (#4013)
- *An Incomplete Guide to the Future* by Willis W. Harman (#4012)
- *Murder and Madness* by Donald T. Lunde, M.D. (#4010)
- *The Anxious Economy* by Ezra Solomon (#4009)
- *The Galactic Club: Intelligent Life in Outer Space* by Ronald Bracewell (#4008)
- *Is Man Incomprehensible to Man?* by Philip H. Rhinelander (#4005)
- *Some Must Watch While Some Must Sleep* by William E. Dement, M.D. (#4003)
- *Human Sexuality: Sense and Nonsense* by Herant Katchadourian, M.D. (#4002)